T-202

Mrs Jack W. Berger

Jerusalem

NEW ASPECTS OF ARCHAEOLOGY

Edited by Sir Mortimer Wheeler

Jerusalem

Excavating 3000 Years of History

Kathleen M. Kenyon

21 Color Plates
92 Monochrome Plates
16 Line Drawings

McGRAW-HILL BOOK COMPANY

NEW YORK TORONTO LONDON SYDNEY

Contents

THE CAMPAIGN OF EXCAVATIONS which has revealed the history of Jerusalem is approaching completion in the current year, 1967, the centenary of the first large-scale investigation of the archaeology of the city. The pioneers of 1867 and their successors of the 1890's excavated by shaft and tunnel. Their results were remarkable and their reports a monument to their courage, persistence and scholarship. But archaeological exploration at that stage was in its infancy. The idea of dating structures by their relation to their contemporary surfaces and the dating of these associated layers was only developing in England at the end of the century, and the new scientific approach was slow to spread to the Mediterranean area. The shafts and tunnels of Warren in 1867 and Bliss and Dickie in 1894–7 could never *date* walls, though they discovered them in circumstances which would daunt us today. Their successors in the first third of the twentieth century still had not fully mastered the techniques of dealing with the very difficult problems of a site like Jerusalem. The historian of the 1950's had to recognize that his theories of the growth of Jerusalem were based on very unsound ground. He could invoke historical and topographical reasoning to support them, but he could not invoke any sound archaeological fact.

It was against this background that the British School of Archaeology in Jerusalem initiated a new campaign of excavations in 1961 and has continued them for seven seasons. The School proposed the project not only because it was recognized that the problem of the history of Jerusalem was the most important outstanding one in Palestinian archaeology but because there was an immediate urgency demanding that it should be tackled. For nearly two millennia Jerusalem had been confined within the walls of the present Old City, of which the medieval walls, complete in their circuit, and gates built by Suleiman the Magnificent in the sixteenth century, form the great charm of the city today. Only under the British Mandate from 1919 did a new City of any size begin to grow up outside the walls. This was mainly to the west, and with the partition of 1948 was included in Israel. The growth of the Jordanian New City then began, at first extending to the north. But by 1960 it was becoming apparent that growth was beginning to the south too, in the area which had been included within the walls of Jerusalem at earlier stages. If the problems of these earlier stages were to be solved, attack on them could not be long delayed. In the event it is clear that if the start of the excavations had been delayed even five years, much of the evidence we have recovered would have been unobtainable.

The project was of course dependent on local support and interest. From the top to the bottom this has been generously and willingly given. His Majesty King Hussein expressed his interest and full support. Official approval was given by the Government of the Hashemite Kingdom of Jordan on the advice of the Department of Antiquities and the expedition owes everything to the continuing interest of the Department and its Director Dr Awni Dajani. Successive Governors of Jerusalem, especially H. E. Anwar Nuseibi, enabled all political, military and police difficulties to be overcome, a support and interest absolutely essential when part of our work was carried out on the very frontiers of Jordan. Our greatest and most long-continuing friend was the Lord Mayor, Rawhi Khatib, and if he could not deal with particular problems himself, he passed us on to the City Engineer Yussef Budeiri. Ready at hand was also the Palestine Archaeological Museum and its Curator, Yussef Saad, with help over equipment and the provision of its excellent lecture-theatre for the presentation of the annual report.

Permission to excavate had to be obtained from numerous owners. The permission of private owners presented only the problems of negotiation of rent and perquisites. But we owe a great debt to all the great religious communities owning land in and around Jerusalem which without exception most generously gave us permission to dig up their land: the supreme Moslem Awqaf, the Greek Patriarchate, the Armenian Patriarchate, and the Anglican Archbishopric. Finally, the Order of St John of Jerusalem allowed us to excavate a vital area in the heart of the Old City.

The enterprise was clearly an enormous one, for the area to be investigated covered a square mile or more, with lesser investigations further afield. Appropriately, the exploration of Jerusalem has over the years been international. The major investigations have been British, but the continuous link has been French, since the Dominican École Biblique et Archéologique de St Étienne has kept careful watch and directed a critical scholarly attention on all finds; and the name of Père Hugues Vincent, O. P., will always be associated with the archaeology of Jerusalem. It was therefore a great satisfaction that the École willingly agreed to join the British School and to be associated with the first three years of the excavations, with Père Roland de Vaux, O. P., as co-Director. In the second season the two Schools were joined as sponsors by the Royal Ontario Museum, led by Dr A. D. Tushingham, and the Canadian collaboration has continued throughout.

Even with these sponsors, the task of raising adequate finance was a heavy one. The École Biblique received a grant from the Commission des Fouilles of the French Government. The Royal Ontario Museum was supported by the University of Toronto and over the years most of its other academic institutions, Victoria University, the University of Trinity College, the University of St Michael's College (Faculty of Divinity), Knox College, University College and McGill University. The United Kingdom support came from many sources.

Three institutions were associated in the enterprise, the British School of Archaeology in Jerusalem, the Palestine Exploration Fund, the initiator of the whole century of excavation, and the British Academy. The B.S.A.J. and the P.E.F. contributed according to their modest means, but the major support came in an ever-increasing scale from the British Academy; without the Academy the dig would have been impossible. Outside the Academy, the greatest United Kingdom support came from the Russell Trust, to which a great debt of gratitude is due. Lesser, but very welcome since so faithful, support came from Birmingham City Museum, the Ashmolean Museum, the Universities of Oxford, Cambridge, London, Glasgow, Durham, Liverpool, Sheffield and Trinity College, Dublin, and a number of other institutions and private individuals. But international support was not limited to that of the United Kingdom, French and Canadian sponsors. The National Geographic Society of America has made a very substantial Research Grant from 1962 to 1966. Other American contributions have come from Emory University, Georgia, the Southern Baptist Seminary, Louisville, and the Pennsylvania Museum. Further afield, contributions have come from the University of Sydney, the Australian Institute of Archaeology, Melbourne, and Otago Museum, New Zealand. This list is not exhaustive, but it indicates the wide base of support given to the enterprise. The budget of some £ 11,000 per annum in the later years shows the need for such world support.

An excavation such as this is very much a corporate affair. A very large number of assistants and students has taken part, coming from many countries. The greater number have of course come from the countries of the three sponsoring bodies, the United Kingdom, France and Canada. But to them are to be added those from our host-country Jordan, the U.S.A., Australia, New Zealand, Denmark, Holland, Belgium, Spain, Germany, Argentina, Japan and Saudi Arabia. Finally and basically, of course, comes our great army of labourers, the bulk, rising to 525 in 1966, from the Jerusalem neighbourhood, headed by our invaluable foreman, Abdul Jewad Abbassi, but with a very important leavening of highly trained experts who began their archaeological career in the School's excavations at Jericho and continued to Jerusalem.

It is on the results of these excavations, based over the years on such wide-scale support, and carried out by the energy and enthusiasm of such a large staff, that the history of Jerusalem is re-written in this book.

I

Introduction

JERUSALEM TODAY consists of an Old City and two new cities. The Old City is the lineal descendant of the medieval city, preserving many of its features and above all still enclosed by the majestic circuit of walls built by Suleiman the Magnificent in 1535. The two new cities have been divided by the Demilitarized Zone that is the relic of the fighting at the end of the British Mandate in 1948, the Israeli-occupied part, which covers the area of the New City that grew up in the time of the Mandate, lapping the walls of the Old City on the west, the Arab city extending north from the north walls. Fortunately for archaeology and history, both areas lie outside the town of all earlier periods, and will not concern us here.

The Old City is still densely populated, and its quarter of a square mile of area has formed the nucleus of Jerusalem for two thousand years, but since it is a living city, it affords very little opportunity for archaeological investigation. It is therefore fortunate that much of that Jerusalem that preceded the present Old City by nearly another two thousand years lies further to the south. Like every town in hill-country, Jerusalem's plan and history have been controlled by topography, and this must first be described.

Plate 1

An air view gives the Old City the aspect of a plateau limited by valleys to the east and west. But a walk through its streets soon shows one that down its centre runs a pronounced hollow from which one climbs up to the Haram esh-Sherif to the east or the Citadel to the west. This hollow represents an actual valley, the steepness of the contours of which is masked by the age-long accumulation of debris. Something of its original shape is shown by the transverse section

drawn by Warren on the basis of the soundings made in 1867[1]. The
central valley, called the Tyropoeon by the Jewish historian Josephus,
divides the site of Jerusalem into two ridges. The eastern ridge is
bounded on the east by the valley today called Silwan, or Siloam,
the ancient Kedron, which is the continuation of the valley that curves
round from the north to cut off the site from Mount Scopus and
the Mount of Olives. It begins to become deep and steep at the point
where the Old City is built on its lip, and it drops steadily and narrows
markedly beyond the southern limits of the Old City. Nine hundred
metres south of these limits, it is joined by the central valley, making a
V-shaped end to the eastern ridge, the crest of which is for the most
part no more than 100 to 150 metres wide.

Fig. 1

Plate 1
Plate 3

Plate III

The western ridge is both higher and wider. On the west it is
bounded by the Hinnom (or Gehenna) valley, which curves round
to the east to form the southern boundary as well. The Hinnom enters
the Kedron at a point 200 metres south of the confluence of the
Tyropoeon, in such a way that the tip of the western ridge overlaps
that of the eastern ridge.

Plate 2

Plate 3

The southern end of each ridge is sharply defined by steep valleys.
To the north there is no limiting physical feature, and the ridges merge
into the main mass of the line of hill, some 760 metres high at this
point, that forms the backbone of Palestine. The northern boundary
of the town was thus not dictated by geography, and its position has
shifted from time to time. But though the town at no time lay astride
the vital north-south route along the backbone of the country, but
on this spur projecting from it, the importance of Jerusalem from
probably the third millennium onwards lies in the fact that it could
control this route.

The exploration of Jerusalem by excavation has been going on for
a century. When the Palestine Exploration Fund was founded in
1865, the first object of its researches was Jerusalem, and with the
excavations of Captain Charles Warren in 1867[2] there began a long

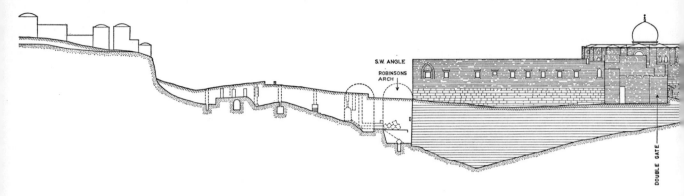

1 *A section showing the two ridges upon which Jerusalem is built and the central valley between, compiled by Warren as the result of his soundings in 1867*

series of expeditions under the auspices of the Palestine Exploration Fund and its daughter organization the British School of Archaeology in Jerusalem, whilst others took place under French, German and Palestinian direction. As early as Warren's excavations in the 1860's, it became clear that early remains stretched south from the present Old City. The full extent of these walls was traced by Bliss and Dickie in their excavations between 1894 and 1897[3]. Their plan has for long been accepted as representing that part of ancient Jerusalem that lay outside the Old City.

The importance of the division of this area into two ridges has long been recognized. Though the central valley is much filled up, the excavations of Warren from 1867[4] onwards and J. W. Crowfoot in 1927[5], showed that in depth and steepness it rivalled the Kedron and the Hinnom. Since Josephus called the western ridge Mount Zion, it was at first believed that the original settlement was there. But there was a cogent reason for expecting that the earliest Jerusalem would be on the eastern ridge, known to Josephus as Ophel, and for many years archaeologists, led by Père Hugues Vincent, who during a long period at the École Biblique et Archéologique de St Etienne became

Fig. 2

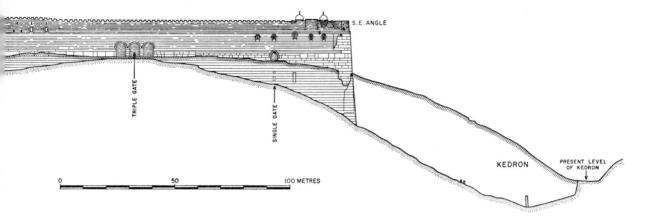

the great repository of all knowledge about Jerusalem, have accepted Ophel as the site of the first Jerusalem.

The reason that the smaller and lower eastern ridge was selected by the first occupants was the elementary one of water supply. From Roman and probably earlier times onward, water could be brought to a site by aqueduct. From the first millennium BC onwards, after lime-mortar had been invented, water from the winter's rainfall could be stored in cisterns, though in a country in which the winter rains may fail for several years in succession, it would be dangerous to rely entirely on cisterns. But before the invention of lime-mortar, cisterns were still less reliable, for mud-mortar is not really impermeable, and water stored in cisterns of this material would not last very long. Every town and village of the Bronze Age and earlier had therefore to be within reach of running water.

The sources of running water in Jerusalem lie in the Kedron valley. There are two springs, known today as 'Ain Umm el Daraj' or the Spring of the Mother of Steps, and Bir 'Ayub, or the well of Job. The latter lies somewhat south of the two ridges, and it would have been impossible to assure access to it in times of trouble. The former, the

Plate II

spring Gihon of the Old Testament and to Christians the Virgin's Fountain, lies at the foot of the eastern ridge, some 325 metres north of its southern extremity, and it was this that made settlement here possible.

Plates 3, 5, 6

Topography therefore indicated that the nucleus of ancient Jerusalem was to be found on the eastern ridge. At some stage, on the evidence of the walls discovered in the course of a hundred years of excavation, the town was expanded to embrace the western ridge, with a wall running from the tip of the eastern ridge across the central valley, and following the curve of the Hinnom round to the southwest corner of the present walls. The archaeological problem was the date of the expansion, for the excavation methods of the last century were not sufficiently precise to provide the evidence.

Fig. 2

Topography and previous archaeological discoveries had provided a basis for further excavation. The evidence of written history must also form the background of any archaeological work, for the Biblical record provides better documentation for Jerusalem than can be claimed for any other city in Western Asia. Jerusalem's appearance in written history in fact precedes the earliest surviving Biblical records by some centuries, for it is one of the towns that figure in the Amarna Letters. These letters, covering a period *c.* 1390 to 1360 BC, are from rulers of towns in Syria and Palestine to the Egyptian government, at a time when, under Akhenaten, the dominance of Egypt in the area was weakening, and when peace and security were being threatened by the attacks of roving warlike bands, the Khabiru, amongst whom the ancestors of the Hebrews may well have been included. Among the towns loyal to Egypt from which the appeals came was Jerusalem, ruled by a certain Abd-Khiba[6].

Plate 4

2   *The plan published by Bliss and Dickie in 1898 which up till 1961 was believed to indicate the plan of Jerusalem in the time of the Kingdom of Judah*

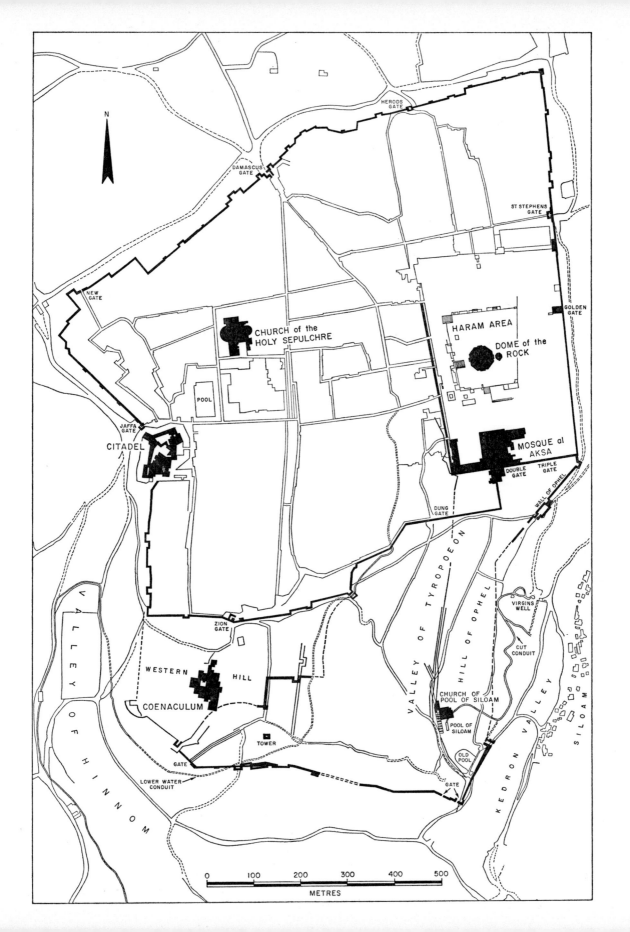

This period of the fourteenth century marks the beginning of the infiltration into Palestine of allied groups which were, in the interpretation generally accepted by modern scholars, ultimately to coalesce as the Israelites. The Biblical evidence supports that of the Amarna Letters in showing that Jerusalem opposed the newcomers, and in the Book of Joshua it is clear that the opposition was successful, for *Joshua 15.63* says 'But the Jebusites, the inhabitants of Jerusalem, the people of Judah could not drive out; so the Jebusites dwell with the people of Judah at Jerusalem to this day.' Jerusalem did not fall to the Israelites until the time of David, from which the great strength of the site can be inferred.

The Jerusalem of the Jebusites and of David

WHEN EXCAVATIONS WERE RENEWED in 1961, ancient Jerusalem was considered to occupy the eastern ridge. Here, a line of walls had been found in earlier excavations, starting with Warren in 1867[7], and continued by Professor Macalister in 1923 to 1926[8]. They followed the crest of the ridge, from the south-east angle of the Temple, and a length is today visible beside the modern road, together with a further length, that cleared by Professor Macalister, 300 metres south of the temple angle, while for the intervening distance their position is indicated by the modern houses that follow the line of the crest. Further fragments of walls picked up at intervals carry the line to the southern tip of the eastern ridge, where it is joined by the wall traced by Bliss and Dickie encircling the western and southern end of the western ridge and crossing the central valley. The walls along the eastern ridge were considered to be the original ones, joined by Bliss and Dickie's wall when the town was extended. Based on this identification, Professor Macalister[9] named a massive tower that he uncovered the Tower of David, which he considered to be a strengthening of the Jebusite defences.

Plate 5

Plates 7, 8

To David, the capture of the Jebusite stronghold was essential, for its position controlling the route along the spine of the hill-country, already mentioned, meant that until he was master there he could not unite the northern and southern tribes into a single kingdom.

David's attack on Jerusalem was made *c.* 996 BC. The Jebusite inhabitants were very confident in the strength of their defences, and they jeered at their attackers and said, 'You will not come in here, but the blind and the lame will ward you off'—thinking 'David

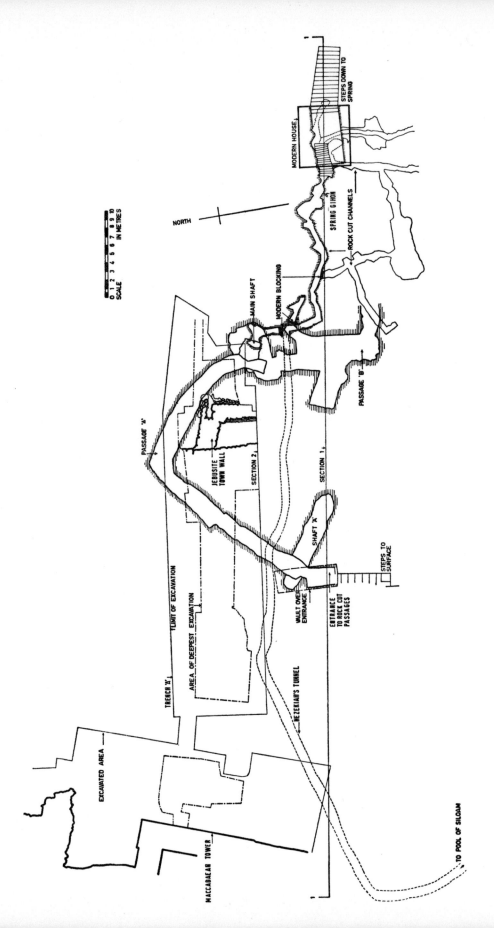

SCALE
0 1 2 3 4 5 6 7 8 9 10
IN METRES

NORTH

MODERN HOUSE

STEPS DOWN TO SPRING

SPRING GIHON

ROCK CUT CHANNELS

MAIN SHAFT

MODERN BLOCKING

PASSAGE 'A'

JEBUSITE TOWN WALL

SECTION 2

PASSAGE 'B'

SECTION 1

SHAFT 'X'

STEPS TO SURFACE

VAULT OVER ENTRANCE

ENTRANCE TO ROCK CUT PASSAGES

TRENCH 'X'

LIMIT OF EXCAVATION

AREA OF DEEPEST EXCAVATION

HEZEKIAH'S TUNNEL

EXCAVATED AREA

MACCABAEAN TOWER

TO POOL OF SILOAM

3 Plan of the Jebusite rock-cut water channel, shaft and tunnel which provided access in wartime to the spring in the valley. The angular course of the tunnel was presumably to reduce the steepness of the route

4 Section of the Jebusite approach to the spring. The view of the tunnel is of course foreshortened, and made to look more steep, because of its angular course. The left-hand shaft was an abortive effort to reach the level of the spring, apparently frustrated by difficult rock conditions

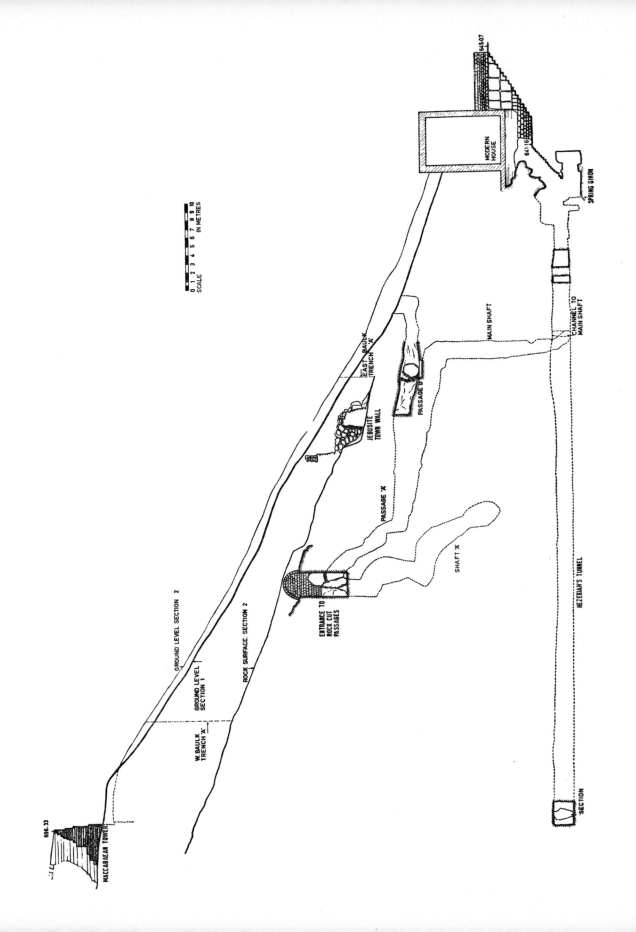

cannot come in here'. The walls were apparently so strong that direct storming was impossible, and David only achieved the capture by a stratagem, which apparently involved a party penetrating within the walls by the route that provided access to the spring. The textual record[11] is somewhat obscure, but that is apparently the meaning of the passage in which Joab led the party whose successful penetration resulted in the capture of the town.

It is clear that there must have been means of access to the spring from within the walls, for the spring lies so low in the valley that a town wall enclosing it would have been commanded by the slope on the opposite side. Therefore, safe access in times of war required a tunnel leading to a shaft coming up inside the town. Such watershafts are familiar in Palestine, the best known being that at Megiddo[12].

Plates 39–42, VIII

A maze of tunnels is in fact connected with the Jerusalem spring. The most famous is the Siloam Tunnel, dating from 700 BC, which still today carries the water through the ridge into the central valley. When, in the course of excavations in 1911, the Siloam Tunnel was cleaned out, Père Vincent[13] made a study of the other tunnels, and

Figs 3, 4

was able to identify the earliest, which consisted of a water channel to the foot of a vertical shaft, from the head of which a sloping passage led to steps to the surface, almost due west of the spring. The devious route of the passage with its sharp angle was presumably to reduce its steepness. The section shows that a first attempt to sink a shaft failed because of the hardness of a seam in the rock.

This, therefore, must have been the means by which the Jebusites obtained water in times of danger. The Biblical account implies, however, that the attacking Israelites discovered the tunnel, and this would have been the route by which Joab entered the city. The upper end of the shaft is no longer visible, for it is covered by a dump from previous excavations, but its position can be fixed from the plan. Even before excavations started, this suggested difficulties concerning the accepted plan of Jebusite Jerusalem. As Figs 3 and 4 show, the position of the head of the shaft lies still some 27 metres outside the line of walls on the crest of the ridge. It would neither have served for safe access to the opening in time of war, nor as a route for attackers to penetrate within the town.

It was for this reason that when excavations began in 1961, the defences in this position on the slope above the spring were made the first point of attack. A trench 11 metres wide and 48 metres long was laid out from the foot of Macalister's 'Tower of David' to a level 27.25 metres lower down.

Plates II, V

It did not take long to establish the negative point that the tower did not belong to the time of David. The previous excavator had cleared the earth against the tower down to the level of the base of the face of the wall, leaving a horizontal surface. Beneath this, he dug a trench along the footings of the tower, exposing a massive stone filling which he took to be the foundations of the tower.

The first point to become apparent was that the horizontal surface is entirely arbitrary, and that the real levels slope down steeply to the east, away from the tower. The next was that the underlying stone filling is the ruins of earlier houses. Further to the north, away from the tower, these houses are better preserved and could be clearly dated. They belong to the seventh century BC, and were destroyed by the Babylonians in 586 BC. It was therefore clear that a tower built over their ruins could not belong to *c.* 1000 BC, and it will appear much later in the story.

Plate 8

The ruins of the seventh century houses project well to the east of the line of wall on the crest. The defences of this period at least therefore lay farther out in this direction, and further down the hill. The answer was therefore to be found in the trench running down the slope. The excavation of this trench was a difficult and unpleasant task. The angle of the surface was nearly 45°. Beneath the scrub and dust of the upper levels was a hardened surface, so steep that it was almost impossible to stand on, still less walk up. Beneath that we

Plate III

Plate 9

reached what was to be the almost universal character of the slope, layer after layer of tumbled stones, medium sized in the higher levels, getting larger as we penetrated further. At the top of the slope, the stones appeared as layers in a soft brown fill, clearly midden tips over the wall on the crest. Lower down, the midden layers petered out, and the stones in them combined with lower layers of rubble to make one vast stony fill. Preserving even an approximately vertical face in such a deposit was almost impossible, as the later stages in the trench show.

It took nearly a whole season's work to get through this stone tumble. Eventually, very massive stone buildings started to appear, with associated pottery of the seventh century BC. These clearly, however, did not belong to lines of defence, and they continued on down the hill. Only at the very end of the season and in the very last foot of the trench did something different appear. It was even more massive in character than the structures hitherto encountered, built of rough *wadi* boulders of great size. But the most important thing about it was its date. It was built slightly in advance of a scarp in the natural rock and between the rock face and the wall was a filling containing only Middle Bronze Age pottery, about 1800 BC.

Plate 10

Here at last it looked as though we had the wall of Jebusite Jerusalem.

Plate VI
Plate 11

To confirm this, it was necessary to continue down the slope, and this was done in 1962. The extension proved that this was indeed the limit of the town, and the early wall was shown to be an angle with a return to the west disappearing under a successor. It proved, moreover, that not only was it the wall of Jebusite Jerusalem but it remained the town wall under David and for several hundred years afterwards, for the rock at its foot was kept clear until about the beginning of the seventh century BC, when it was superseded by the wall that crosses its top.

Plate III

The position of the wall is some two-thirds of the way down the slope. It could not be placed at the foot of the slope so as to bring the spring actually inside the walls, for in that position it would have been commanded by the other side of the narrow valley. A protected access to the spring in times of danger was therefore still necessary. This was provided by the tunnel and shaft already described, which a wall located as revealed by the excavations would protect perfectly satisfactorily.

Though the portion of the original town wall was excavated in 1961 and 1962, it remains the only portion completely exposed. In excavating on a slope like this, it is no light matter to extend a trench. Excavating to the depth of the early wall means excavating to a depth of *c.* 5 metres. In the first stages too, it meant removing the dump beside the original trench, with the additional problem of constructing a revetting wall for the dump higher up the trench. A further complication was that the line of the later wall proved to run somewhat obliquely, and the first area cleared failed to expose its face, so once again the process of clearing dump from the upper slopes had to be carried out. The completion of this clearance of the lower levels must await another season.

This first trench gave us evidence of the line of the early defences on the east side. The line on the north side has been indicated with some certainty, though the actual wall has not yet been exposed. Its position is bracketed by Sites H on the north and P on the south on the plan. Site H covered one of the few areas on the crest of the ridge available for excavation. The area immediately to the south had been excavated in 1923–6, while much of the rest of it is either built over or cut into narrow garden strips with olive and fig trees, very expensive to destroy, for one has to pay to the owners a highly notional valuation. Moreover, in the comparatively shallow depth of accumulation on the summit, Byzantine and Arab foundation-walls and cisterns have played havoc with the evidence of earlier occupation. However, Site H did produce a few areas of intact stratification, and their evidence was unambiguous. There was no occupation here until

Fig. 5

about the tenth century BC. Therefore this part of the summit lay outside the Jebusite town, and probably outside that of the time of David, though the chronology of pottery is not yet so precise as to render it possible to make a definite statement on this point.

Site H also gave hints that there was an important wall crossing the ridge from east to west at this point. Unfortunately, it ran along the southern border, coinciding on one side with the property boundary, beyond which evidence had been destroyed by the 1923–6 excavation, in which stratification had not been observed, while on the northern side of the wall was a path with a water-pipe. The wall itself was clearly of more than one period, but it was so wide that it completely filled the strip available between the path and property boundary, and it was therefore not possible to obtain stratigraphical evidence of its date. A substitute for the missing evidence came from Site P. Here, though the area had been trenched in 1923–6, excavation had not been carried to bed-rock. The lowest deposits were in complete contrast to those in Site H, for the pottery in them was entirely of the Late Bronze Age, of the fourteenth to thirteenth centuries BC. Thus a strip some 8 metres wide, largely occupied by a heavy wall, divided an area which was within the Jebusite town from one which was outside it. One can therefore draw a line across the hill on the map at this point with some certainty.

Today there does not appear to be any obvious reason for placing the original north wall at that point. The modern surface levels rise gradually and steadily to the north, and the flat area of the surface of the ridge gradually widens. But the modern crest of the eastern slope does not correspond with the natural crest. This was proved in Site R, 37 metres north of Site H. In the latter site, rock was reached on the crest at 4 metres from the surface. In Site R, it had not been reached at a depth of 8.79 metres from the surface, beyond which point it was not possible to excavate owing to the instability of the soil. Where rock was reached on the western side of the area cleared in the strip

Fig. 5

along the eastern edge, where alone excavation is complete, it was at 8.60 metres from the surface. The rock summit of the ridge was therefore not rising and widening like the modern surface, but at this point was narrower and lower. It would seem that somewhere north of Site H, either between it and Site R, or at Site R, there was a constriction of the ridge which dictated the position of the original north wall.

The place where the west wall was to be sought was indicated in the first place by negative evidence. In the first excavation season in 1961, a number of sites were excavated on the south-east slopes of the western ridge, Sites B, D, D 2, E and F. The evidence from all of them was similar. There was no occupation in this area until the first century AD, and the evidence from Site F, to which we shall return, proved that the town-wall shown on the plan of the 1894–7 excavations belongs only to that period. At least the southern end of the western ridge, therefore, was not included within the walls until then.

The west wall of early Jerusalem was therefore to be sought on the western side of the eastern ridge. A hint to this effect had already been given in the excavations of J. W. Crowfoot in 1927. At his site south of Site M, he found a massive wall and gateway that was certainly in use in the Maccabean period, in the last centuries BC. In the context of the then generally accepted view that the western hill had been brought within the town long previously, such a wall in this period was difficult to explain, but it fits in perfectly with the 1961 evidence concerning the western hill.

Crowfoot believed that the massive scale and rough masonry of this wall indicated an original construction in the Bronze Age. As will be seen, there is no longer any reason for such a postulation. Crowfoot's wall is appreciably down the slope of the western side of the rock. The present evidence makes it clear that the original wall was higher up the slope. The first effort to find it, in Site M, produced the unsatisfactory results with which excavations in Jerusalem have

Fig. 5

made us all too familiar. This site lies immediately west of the road that here runs along the western edge of the summit. A strip was excavated immediately beside the road. This showed that not only all the earliest occupation deposits had disappeared, but also even the original surface of the rock. At some stage, likely, as will be seen, to have been in the Roman period, the whole of the rock-surface had been quarried. The first surviving occupation consisted of houses of the Byzantine period, and great cisterns and baths of that period added to the preceding destruction.

Fig. 5

This first strip of Site M, therefore, gave us no indication of the line of the early wall. An extension west of Site M is too far north to be expected to provide evidence of the earliest period, for it lies north of the position of the north wall suggested by Sites H and P. So it proved; there was nothing here of the Jebusite or Davidic period, though, as will be seen, there is some evidence concerning the Solomonic period. However, though the excavation is not yet complete, it has already shown that the extension of the town down the slope belongs only to the Maccabean period. The evidence will be described in Chapter VII.

Further south, Site K produced similar evidence limiting the extent of the early town on the west site. This site is now a terrace between a pronounced rock scarp marking the summit of the ridge, here very narrow, and the same road running down the valley that has been mentioned in connection with Site M. Excavation showed that the only traces of early occupation consisted of one or two pockets of Iron Age pottery in crevices in the rock, and there was nothing at all belonging to the Bronze Age. The original wall must therefore have followed the line of the summit scarp. There is, however, no hope of finding it, since, as will be seen, the rock on the summit of the ridge was heavily quarried in Roman and Byzantine times.

Excavation has therefore delimited the extent of the earliest town, even if on the north and west sides it has not uncovered any portion

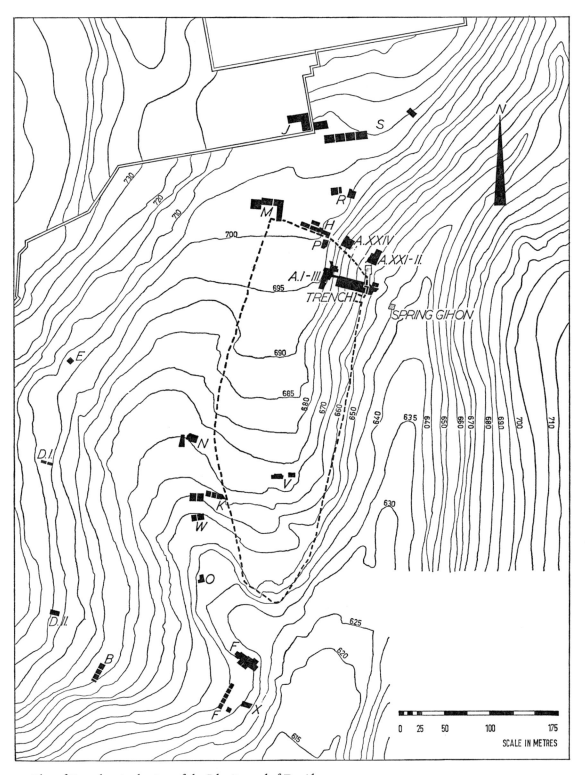

5　*Plan of Jerusalem in the time of the Jebusites and of David*

of the wall. It is therefore possible to draw the plan shown in Fig. 5. The area of the town so delimited is small, only some 10.87 acres. Its importance in the Late Bronze Age and Early Iron Age lay not in its size, but in the strategic position that has already been described (p. 13).

One further point about the plan of early Jerusalem emerged in the 1965 season. Though the continuation of the wall found in 1961–2 has not yet been fully uncovered in the depth so far reached, it has already become apparent that the continuation is built against the angle already cleared. That is to say, the wall is not built in a series of offsets and insets. Instead, the angle is a tower, projecting both forwards and backwards from the main line of the wall. Towers may of course be incorporated at any point in a wall. But when one considers the position of this tower, it becomes apparent that it is not a mere interval tower. It is almost certain that it is the tower of a town gate.

This is indicated by its relation to the position of the spring. Our first approach to the problems of the eastern wall of Jerusalem in the early periods was guided by the need to explain the relation of the first shaft and tunnel to the contemporary defences. This the location of the earliest wall has satisfactorily established. But though this means of hidden and safe access to the water was essential in times of war, it must have been exceedingly inconvenient. In times of peace there must have been access above ground, to an entrance to the spring which would have been blocked and presumably hidden when trouble threatened; even if total concealment could not have been hoped for, the inhabitants might have thought that the difficulties of access up the vertical shaft, without the ropes let down from above which the occupants could have used, would prevent it from endangering their security. The great reward that David offered, which was won by Joab, showed how perilous the route in fact was and the reward commensurate with the peril.

Plate 11

If it is then accepted that there would have been a simpler, everyday, peace-time access, one has only to look at the slope from the opposite side of the valley to see that the spring must almost certainly have been reached by a route from the summit which would have followed closely the line of the path that today descends the slope, passing just to the south of the tower in the early wall. The tower would therefore fit beautifully as the northern tower of a gateway, the rest of which would lie almost exactly beneath the modern path. One can therefore deduce that here was the water-gate of ancient Jerusalem. It has the further interest that it would have been the way by which Solomon came back into the city after he had been anointed at the Spring Gihon[14].

Plate V

The plan of Jerusalem looks very different now, after our five seasons of excavation, from what it had been believed to be before. Limits on the north and west sides can be proposed which were unknown before, and the one line of wall which was believed to be known has been shown to be wrong. This last part is especially revolutionary. In the first place, it adds a width of fifty metres to the plan of the town, at a point where the summit of the ridge apparently limited this width to about a hundred metres. As a bald statement, this does not sound particularly interesting. It is when one comes to consider what adding this area meant that one realizes what it involved. The reason for extending beyond the flat area of the summit in this direction is quite clear, to bring the town as near to the water-supply as was tactically possible. But the area so added to the town is uninviting. The present surface slopes at an angle of nearly 45°, that of the underlying bed-rock at about 25°. This would create problems of lay-out for a town. Only a few traces of the houses belonging to the earliest defences of *c.* 1800 BC survived. They climbed the slope of the hill, following the angle of the rock, and, as might be expected, were small and irregularly planned to accommodate themselves to the slope and its irregularities.

About the fourteenth to thirteenth centuries BC there was a revolutionary town-planning development that made it possible to change what must have been a straggling suburb into a fully built-up part of the town. Starting from the top of the slope, a series of stone-filled platforms was constructed with the object of converting the slope into a number of terraces. The first step was to build retaining-walls parallel to the slope of the hill, that is to say running north and south. Against these walls was piled the fill, in a series of compartments, each of which was faced by a thin wall built on a batter leaning back against the stones of the compartment. These facing walls were much too slender to have any strength, for they were only a single stone thick. They must have been simply a constructional device, to stabilize one section of the fill, and to enable the next section to be piled up against it. A considerable area of this stone filling was examined at the top of the slope. A succession of nine of these compartments was traced, each leaning back against its neighbour to the north. At the northern edge of the area cleared, the apex of this particular part of the construction was apparently reached, with the next compartments to the north beginning to lean back in the opposite direction against this apex. If, as is to be presumed, a considerable part of the slope was built up in this way; presumably the process was started from a number of such cores, and the space between gradually filled up.

It is probable that the total height of the stone filling nowhere survives. The maximum exposed was 6 metres, but a little way off the upper part of a compartment belonging to the same complex was uncovered, and this stood some 4.45 metres higher. It is quite possible that this particular platform stood at least to that height. Though there can be doubt as to the original height of the platforms, it is completely certain that none of the buildings first constructed on top of them survive. The original date of construction is given by the potsherds in the fill. They are somewhat meagre both in number and size, but they are enough to show that the platforms were constructed in the

1 Air view of Jerusalem from the south-west, taken before the 1939–45 war. The closely built-up area of the Old City is surrounded by walls erected in their present form by Suleiman the Magnificent, AD 1535. Excavation has shown that these walls essentially represent those of the Roman city of Aelia Capitolina of the second century AD. The Old City is dominated by the great platform of the Haram esh-Sherif, in the centre of which is the Dome of the Rock. This platform was constructed by Herod the Great at the end of the first century BC to support the rebuilt Temple, on the site of Solomon's Temple. To the east *(right)*, the city is bounded by the Kedron valley. To the west is the Hinnom valley, which curves round to join the Kedron just off the picture. South of the Old City, the two ridges upon which it was built become apparent, though the central valley, the Tyropoeon, is much silted up. The original Jerusalem lay on the eastern of the two ridges so formed

2 The valley of the Hinnom from the north-east, seen from the southern end of the western ridge. It has here curved round to run in an easterly direction to join the Kedron. This valley is the Biblical Gehenna, a polluted place where dead animals were thrown and rubbish burnt. From its unsavoury associations and the pall of smoke that hung over it, it became allegorically the place of punishment of the wicked

3 Jerusalem from the south. In the background, the walls of the Old City. To the right of the south-east corner of the Temple platform is the Kedron valley, bounding the eastern ridge on the east. The great mass of trees in the foreground marks the junction of the Kedron and the Hinnom, which disappears behind the bluff on the left. The spur of trees running up to the north-west marks the line of the Tyropoeon, which forms the western boundary of the eastern ridge. The narrow promontory between this and the Kedron was the site of the earliest Jerusalem

4 One of the Amarna tablets written by Abdi-Kheba, ruler of Jerusalem, to the Egyptian Pharaoh Amenophis IV (Akhenaten) (1376–1359 BC), imploring help from the raiding Khabiru, and accusing his neighbours of disloyalty and of encouraging the enemy. The letters are written in cuneiform, in the Akkadian (Babylonian) language, which was the diplomatic *lingua franca*, but most of the scribes were Canaanites with an imperfect knowledge of the language (p. 16)

5   The site of Jerusalem, from the east. Between the buildings in the foreground, which are part of the village of Silwan, and Jerusalem runs the Kedron valley. The crest of the eastern ridge runs from the south-east corner of the Temple, and the line of houses marks the line of the wall hitherto supposed to be that of Old Testament Jerusalem

6   Looking down the Kedron valley from the north-east. The line of the road on the right and the houses which continue from it along the crest of the ridge mark the line of wall first established by Solomon to link the original city to his Temple, to which the post-Exilic town shrank back. On the left is the main excavation trench, at the lower end of which was found the wall of the Jebusite and Davidic city

7, 8 Part of the defences uncovered in the 1923–5 excavations, in which the tower was ascribed to the work of David and Solomon. In the foreground of the upper view is shown the massive structure, built in a series of steps, which the 1923–5 excavators believed to be a bastion in the Jebusite defences. As the lower view shows, the tower was in fact built on top of the ruins of houses of the seventh century BC (*see* Plates 47–50), destroyed by the Babylonians in 586 BC. The tower therefore has nothing to do with the time of David. It proved to belong to the second century BC. Its contemporary surface is the sloping line in the background. The so-called bastion is later than the tower, and represents a patch, covered by the contemporary surface, in the Maccabean defences (pp. 23, 115)

9 The trench cut down the surface of the steep slope from the foot of the tower (Plates 7 and 8), in
search of the true east wall of the original town of Jerusalem, encountered in its early stages this terrible
tumble of stones. The tumble in places was as much as 5 metres deep. The first stages represented the
collapse of the terraces which had been built upon this slope *(see* Plates 12 and 13) when the city was
destroyed by the Babylonians in 586 BC. When the walls were rebuilt by Nehemiah *c.* 440 BC, this area
was left outside the city, with the walls on the crest of the slope. They too suffered several destructions
and collapse, and each of these added to the tumble of stones. In the edge of the trench, and in the key
left standing in the centre can be seen a series of smooth surfaces. They probably represent a tidying-up
of the slope in the time of Herod the Great, making a very steep glacis-like surface almost impossible to
climb, as was only too clear to the excavators who had to clean them (p. 24)

10, 11   At the lower end of the great trench down the slope, the east wall of the original Jerusalem was at last reached. The top view shows how its inner side was only just touched in the original trench, while the lower view shows it as exposed in the 1962 extension. It is either a salient in the wall or, more probably, a tower of a gate leading out to the spring at the foot of the slope. It was built originally *c.* 1800 BC, as the wall of the Jebusite stronghold, but was re-used by David and his successors. It was only replaced by the wall on the right in the eighth century BC (pp. 24–5)

12, 13   The slope of the rock above the wall shown in Plates 10 and 11 was exceedingly steep. This uninviting area was included in the Jebusite town in order to place the town wall sufficiently low on the slope to control the spring in the valley *(see* Plate III). The original buildings following the rock surface on this slope were necessarily small and irregular. In the fourteenth–thirteenth century BC there was a great town-planning operation, in which the slope was built up in a series of terraces. Behind a succession of retaining walls were stone-filled compartments, faced by slender walls built on a batter (Plates 12, IV). These substructures provided flat terraces upon which much better planned houses could be built. The terraces were however very vulnerable to destruction by earthquake, heavy rain or enemy action. Plate 13 shows how they collapsed, in this case to the south, with evidence of at least three repairs within the Jebusite period. At the bottom of Plate 13 are walls of the earlier period, built on bedrock, which is just visible in the foreground (pp. 32, 49)

14   The great collapse on the eastern slopes, seen in Plates 9 and V shows how all the early buildings inside the walls have disappeared. The buildings on the summit of the ridge have disappeared for other reasons. The main one is that after the destruction of Jerusalem by Titus in AD 70, the area of the original city was left in ruins, and when the Roman city was built in AD 135, this area was used as a quarry. The view, *above*, shows the area excavated in 1913–14, with a maze of cisterns, baths and other rock-cut structures truncated by the quarrying

15   The south-east corner of the Herodian Temple platform. It is built out on a great substructure, which goes down 24 metres below the present surface, completely burying the Solomonic Temple platform

16   The Haram esh-Sherif from the west, on the site of the Temple. The Dome of the Rock stands on the highest point above the rock upon which it is suggested stood the Solomonic Altar of Sacrifice. The Temple is believed to have been to the west of this point. The platform of the Haram esh-Sherif is supported by the walls of the platform built by Herod for his reconstruction of the Temple. Solomon's Temple must likewise have stood on a platform, for the rock surface slopes steeply down to the valley on either side, and a platform would have been necessary to provide space for the courts surrounding the Temple and for Solomon's palace which was adjacent to it. But any traces of the Solomonic structures were completely engulfed by Herod's much larger building. The close-packed buildings of the Old City in the foreground may well suggest the appearance of ancient Jerusalem, though the greater part of this area was only included within the town in the time of Herod Agrippa. In the background is the Mount of Olives (p. 55)

17 Photograph of a model showing the rock surface upon which Jerusalem was built, with an outline of the present Old City superimposed *(cf.* the air photograph on Plate 1). To the east *(right)* of the Old City is the Kedron valley, between the Mount of Olives on the right and the site of the city. The Hinnom is seen bounding the city on the west, and curving round to join the Kedron. Between a much broader western ridge and a narrow eastern ridge is a central valley, the Tyropoeon, which curves round, forming the end of the eastern ridge, to join the Kedron just north of the mouth of the Hinnom. The continuance north of the Tyropoeon is masked by the Old City, but it in fact continues right up through the city to the point where the line of the north wall changes angle, and only merges into the main ridge just beyond this point. The Temple therefore stood on the continuation of the narrow eastern ridge, and its platform had on both sides to be supported on great substructure walls, at the south-east corner 46 metres high, at the south-west corner 38 metres high (p. 55)

18, 19 No masonry of the time of Solomon has survived at Jerusalem, but at Samaria, some eighty years later, Omri, like Solomon, employed Phoenician masons. The buildings of Period I at Samaria, dating to *c.* 880 BC are in typical Phoenician masonry. The face of the wall is in most beautiful ashlar blocks, with perfectly fitting joints. The foundation course has irregular bosses left, with one or more margins dressed. The courses consist of headers and stretchers on edge, with the stretchers keying into the core. In the core, the stones are quite rough. In the view, *below*, a rebuild in Period III, mid-ninth century BC, is still in position. This shows the native style of building in rough, undressed blocks, to which the inhabitants reverted when the foreign masons left (pp. 59, 62)

20   A Proto-Ionic (sometimes called Proto-Aeolic) pilaster capital from Jerusalem. It was found broken at the foot of the scarp on the eastern crest of the eastern ridge, with a tumble of ashlar blocks which could have formed part of a wall in the Samaria style (Plates 18 and 19). Similar capitals were found at Samaria, where they may have belonged to Omri's Phoenician style building. Others have been found at Megiddo and Beth-shan, at both of which sites there were buildings of the Solomonic period. This may thus be the sole architectural fragment surviving from Solomon's buildings (p. 59)

21   An orthostat carving of a lion on a basalt block found at Hazor, belonging to the Canaanite temple illustrated in Plates 22, 23. It probably stood as a guard to the porch, but was found in a pit dug into the floors of the earlier temple. It is not certain whether it was discarded by the builders of the second temple or whether for ritual motives the destroyers of the second temple had buried it. The body is in bas-relief, but the head is in the round. This is a style typical of Hittite regions and may be an example of Hittite influences in Northern Palestine, to which at times Hittite political power extended

22, 23 Solomon's temple at Jerusalem was on a familiar Semitic plan, with a porch leading to a main hall, with a holy of holies beyond, though it was much grander and more elaborate than any other known buildings. A good example of this plan has been found at Hazor, here illustrated. There were two stages, both within the Late Bronze Age, belonging probably to the fourteenth and thirteenth centuries BC. In the upper view, the porch is in the foreground, with the basalt bases of two columns flanking the entrance into the main hall, beyond which is the entrance into the holy of holies. The view, *below*, is of the holy of holies in the second stage, and shows some of the ceremonial equipment, displaced and overturned, which may serve as examples, on a small scale, of the equipment of Solomon's temple described in the Bible. Lying on its back near the centre is a basalt incense altar which on the front, the upper side as it lies, had a disk with a four-rayed star in the centre, identified as the emblem of the Canaanite sun-god. The large vessels visible, of stone and pottery, near which were a number of dipper flasks, presumably held oil or wine for use in the temple ritual. There was also a statue of a seated man holding a goblet (p. 60)

24 In the court of Solomon's temple there were, in addition to the altar of burnt offerings, a number of ritual furnishings. These included twelve lavers of bronze. They rested on wheeled carriers of bronze, Phoenician in character. Of these the most notable come from Cyprus. The one here illustrated is almost exactly comparable with a stand from Megiddo, of which the period may be close to the time of Solomon, though it apparently lacked wheels (p. 60)

second half of the Late Bronze Age, fourteenth to thirteenth centuries BC. In the area excavated, nothing of the contemporary overlying buildings survived on the greater part of the slope of the hill. Buildings were however found at the top of the slope, but they were separated in date by five hundred years or more from the period of the platforms.

The reason for this gap lies in the nature of the construction. The whole stability of the lay-out depended in fact on the retaining walls running parallel to the slope of the hill, for they took the thrust of the fill behind them. Each in turn was supported by other walls and terraces down the hill, perhaps in sequence ultimately to the town wall, though there has been too much destruction to show this. A breach or collapse at any point in the system would have disastrous consequences, for its effects would rapidly spread to the terraces above it, and the collapse of each terrace wall would bring the houses on the terrace tumbling down the slope. Breaches could have been caused by enemy action, by an earthquake, or even by the torrential rain that falls in the winter in Jerusalem.

There is in fact visual evidence of a number of collapses in the platforms on the upper part of the slope. The original stone core here survives only towards the base of the platform, and there is stratigraphical evidence of at least four rebuilds.

Plate 13

It has been worth while dwelling at some length on these complicated platform structures, because they explain a good deal about the history of Jerusalem. The Bible records a number of instances of the capture of the town by an enemy. It was clearly all too easy for an enemy to wreak very serious destruction. A mere breach in a town wall would not be difficult to repair. But when such a breach involved a collapse of a considerable area of the town behind it, the danger was much more serious. It is in those terms that we must think of assaults on Jerusalem.

What the excavations have therefore so far established can be described as the skeleton of Jebusite Jerusalem of the second millennium BC, the framework provided by the line of the walls and what, to continue the anatomical analogy, could be thought of as the ribs which supported the body. Of the flesh which would be represented by the houses supported by the basic structures, nothing has survived in the area excavated, and from what the excavations have shown us of the effect on the material remains of natural and human destructive agencies, I would be prepared to wager heavily that nothing can have survived in any other area.

So far as both the literary and the archaeological evidence goes, David seized the Jebusite town and made it his capital, but did not extend it. According to the Biblical record, he repaired Jerusalem, and, especially, he built from *Millo* round and about[15]. As far as the archaeological evidence about the town walls is concerned, though nothing that one can ascribe to David has been found in the one small section of the actual earliest wall that has been uncovered, it is easy to accept the suggestion of the text that David took over the existing walls and merely repaired them, for this section of wall, which it has been suggested (p. 30) formed part of the east gate, remained in use until sometime in the eighth century BC.

The *Millo* appears among the building activities of Solomon and several others of David's successors[16]. Its identification has been the subject of much speculation and ingenuity. The original translators of the Old Testament did not understand what was meant, and simply transcribed the Hebrew original. It is from a Semitic root which has the meaning of filling. Based on this meaning almost every writer on the history of Jerusalem has made his own suggestion—the filling of a breach in the wall, the filling of the central valley to join the eastern ridge to the western, the filling of a transverse ravine believed to limit the town to the north, a tower solidly filled with stone, and so on. The present excavations have produced a new candidate. The stone-filled terraces described above (p. 49) could very justly be described as *Millo*. Their vulnerability and the necessity of keeping them in repair has already been emphasized. It is very probable that they would have been damaged when David captured Jerusalem, particularly since the traditional association of the water-shaft with the capture suggests that the attack was concentrated on the east side. The repair of any damage done would have demanded a high degree of priority, as otherwise an important part of the site would have crumbled away. Succeeding kings would have had to deal with a similar problem. We can feel therefore that we have here a very strong candidate for identification as *Millo*[17].

Plates 29, 30

It may seem disappointing that the excavations have discovered none of the buildings of David's city. It will have become apparent that the city consisted essentially of two parts, that built on the narrow rock spine of the ridge, with the western wall following closely the scarp at the summit of the western valley, and that built on the terraces on the eastern slope. Nothing earlier than the seventh century BC survives on the portion excavated so far. It is likely, owing to the precarious nature of the structures, that none of the earlier remains will have survived anywhere, though other expeditions might happen to light on an intact portion. But on the rock spine it is virtually certain that nothing survives. When excavations began in 1961, quite a considerable part of the summit was free of buildings, though this has become less and less the case every year. Within the area to which we now know that David's city was limited, virtually no area remains in which there is any hope of finds of the period. For a distance of 120 metres south from the northern limit, the whole width of the summit has been excavated by earlier expeditions. A bewildering complex of walls had been found. One here must turn to the difficulties of excavating a site on which the natural building material is stone, quarried from the local rock. Where in the Near East local stone is not available, houses and town walls are built of mud-brick. When they fall down, the bricks revert to mud, and their successors are constructed on top of the resultant mound of debris. In this way a *tell*, or a man-made hill, grows up to mark the site of an ancient settlement. The state of affairs is very different when the local rock produces stone suitable for use in building. When a house falls down, the stones from the debris can be recovered to use again, and it is easier to do this than to quarry new stone. Even in our excavations today, every stone we excavate is carefully set aside by the owners of the land for use in the new houses that one and all are planning to build. So in ancient times the builders of all the successive Jerusalems in the restricted area of the original town used the stones fallen from the houses of their predecessors, and also dug up even the foundations when they encountered them. They also were continually excavating into the bed-rock itself to construct cisterns. The result is the virtual disappearance of all except fragments of the early walls, and the mangling and disturbance of the floor levels and occupation deposits. This is not to say that archaeological evidence cannot survive, in the shape of the robber trenches of the walls, from which the plans can be reconstructed, or of stratigraphical evidence showing where the floor levels must have been, and so on. But the interpretation of such evidence requires a highly sophisticated excavation technique, in which the earlier excavators of Jerusalem had not been trained. They were therefore unable to produce any reliable evidence for dating the fragments of wall that they found, and in fact our present experience suggests that much of what they found belongs to the Byzantine period. The whole of this area must therefore be written off as far as any knowledge of early Jerusalem is concerned, and it must be admitted that even if the area had not been already excavated, our knowledge would still have been scrappy and the remains recovered unimpressive. David's successors have destroyed most of his town.

Further south, the position is even worse. The biggest area excavated here was in 1913–14 and 1923–4. The clearance here was very thorough, and the exposed rock surface is still unencumbered. It shows a vast complex of cisterns and other cuttings which on the basis of style go down to the Hellenistic-Herodian period. But one and all have been truncated by quarrying. In 1965 we excavated two areas in Site V and in both cases the rock had been quarried, in one in the Roman period, probably second century AD, in the other in the Byzantine period. Not far away to the north a great cistern stands exposed as an outline from its summit to its base showing that here the thickness of rock removed was at least 5 metres. As will be seen (p. 185) the whole of this part of ancient Jerusalem was destroyed by Titus in AD 70, and lay outside the next Jerusalem, the Aelia Capitolina built by Hadrian in AD 135. The excavation evidence shows that at least the southern part of the original city became the quarry for the stones from which Aelia Capitolina was built.

Plate 14

David's Jerusalem, and that of the preceding Jebusites, has thus virtually vanished, except for the skeleton which we can claim to have established. One can, however, hazard a guess that David's Jerusalem was not very grand. The origins of David himself were simple, a shepherd turned warrior. Excavation of Palestinian sites has made it very clear that the Israelites entered the country as nomads, infiltrating into the Canaanite towns and villages, and absorbing the culture of the land at a time when this culture, based on the urban civilization of the Middle Bronze Age, was decadent. Under David there came a great political development, the unification of the northern and southern tribes, and the establishment of a hegemony from Damascus in the north to the Gulf of Aqaba in the south. David was much too busy with his conquests to spend time on town building. One may suspect that Jerusalem and the other towns and villages remained unimpressive. The grandeur of Jerusalem came with Solomon.

III

Solomon and the Building of the Temple

DAVID'S CAPTURE OF JERUSALEM had made the unification of the Israelite tribes into a single kingdom a physical possibility by clearing away the obstruction of the alien Jebusites from the one good through route that connected the north and the south. By capturing Jerusalem he had also acquired a town that belonged neither to the northern Israelite tribes nor to Judah in the south; it was his own personal possession, and from it the hitherto united tribes could be ruled. He aimed at affixing a seal to this assertion of the importance of Jerusalem by making it the religious centre. The Ark of Yahweh or the Ark of the Covenant was the central symbol of the worship of Yahweh. It had travelled with the Israelites in their traditional wanderings, and had had many vicissitudes, including capture by the Philistines. David with great ceremony transferred it to Jerusalem from Keriath-jearim, which had been its resting-place after its recovery from the Philistines. His plan was in fact revolutionary. The Ark was portable, and its shelter had hitherto been a tent, as was suitable for the religious symbol of a god of a group of nomads. David planned to give it a permanent home in his own city, and with this in view purchased the threshing floor of Araunah the Jebusite, considered to be a site indicated by the arrest at that point of the pestilence sent by Yahweh in displeasure at David's institution of a census[18]. The prophet Nathan, however, instructed David that it was not Yahweh's will that he should build a temple, and the Ark for the rest of David's lifetime continued to be sheltered by a tent.

It fell therefore to David's son and successor Solomon to consummate David's plan to give the Ark a permanent home. There can be no real doubt as to the site of Solomon's Temple, for there is no significant break in the chain that links it with the site of the Haram esh-Sherif or Dome of the Rock, the glorious Moslem sanctuary that dominates the Old City of Jerusalem today. Solomon's Temple lasted down to the time of the Exile in Babylon that followed the capture of the city by Nebuchadnezzar in 586 BC. Though most of the important inhabitants were carried away to Babylon, the city was not deserted, and the exiles even sent offerings to the ruined Temple. When the first exiles were allowed by the Persian conquerors of Babylon to return *c.* 538 BC, their immediate concern was the rebuilding of the Temple, concerning the site of which no doubt could have risen in this interval. The Post-Exilic Temple suffered damage and destruction at intervals in the next five hundred years, but never obliteration, and it was to render this Post-Exilic Temple more worthy and glorious that Herod the Great built his Temple, beginning in *c.* 20 BC. Much of Herod's work can still be traced in the great platform that supports the Dome of the Rock, so from the present structure back to Solomon there is no real break.

Plate 1

One can therefore be certain of the site of Solomon's Temple, but all structures have disappeared. The Post-Exilic Temple and such parts of Solomon's Temple as had survived to be incorporated in it have quite literally been engulfed by Herod's Temple. The basis of the latter is a tremendous platform, *c.* 480 metres from north to south and 300 metres from east to west. It stands on the same narrow ridge as the original city. The description in *I Kings 6* and *7* makes it clear that the Temple, its courtyards and the associated structures required an artificial platform to produce the required level space. In this it resembled Herod's Temple, but the latter was infinitely more grandiose, and the platform extended further into the flanking valleys. All Solomon's structures were therefore buried and are completely inaccessible within the great infilling which supports the present platform.

Plate 15

Plate 16
Fig. 1

Plate 17

The present south wall of the Temple platform is some 200 metres to the north of the limits of David's city. It can be taken as reasonably certain that in Solomon's time the town was extended to join up with the Temple. The plan is suggested in Fig. 6. The archaeological evidence so far is meagre. At Site H on the plan, occupation levels have been found that could belong to the tenth and ninth centuries BC, to the time of Solomon and his successors, as has already been said (pp. 25–6); the evidence that there was nothing earlier in this area shows that the town only expanded here at this stage. In Site M there was evidence that the town not only expanded northward, but there was some building—out at the west side into the central valley. This came from an earth fill that was added to the west of the rock scarp that marks the edge of the summit of the ridge, which contained pottery of this period. It must have been supported by a wall to the west, which was probably also the town wall. This has however disappeared, and the filling is cut by a much later wall (p. 135). This evidence gives within a fairly narrow margin the position of the west wall of Solomon's extension. The east wall has been drawn from the point where the original wall is presumed to curve round to form the north wall, and thence following the present contours to the present south-east angle of the Temple. It is not however even certain that the extension took in the difficult eastern slope of the ridge. It might have been confined to the summit of the ridge. There certainly was a wall here, along the eastern edge of Site H, of the casemate type of construction, consisting of an inner and outer wall joined by cross walls, that was common from the time of Solomon onwards. Subsequent walls destroyed the dating evidence of this wall and obscured its purpose. It could have enclosed an inner area, an acropolis, or it could have been the town wall itself[20a]. It is possible that further excavation will produce more evidence. Another point of uncertainty is of course the point of junction with the Temple platform. On the plan, the east and west walls are shown running to the south-east and

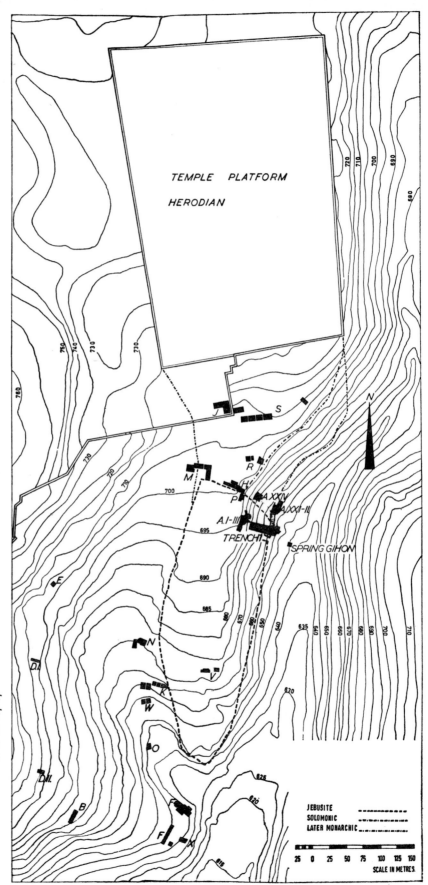

TEMPLE PLATFORM

HERODIAN

*6 Approximate plan of
Jerusalem in the time of
Solomon, with an extension
at the northern end of the
eastern slope made probably
in the eighth century BC*

JEBUSITE
SOLOMONIC
LATER MONARCHIC

25 0 25 50 75 100 125 150
SCALE IN METRES.

north-west corners of the present platform. As has already been said, this platform is bigger than its predecessor, so the original angles may well have been situated further up the hill, and thus the width of the town area may have been less.

The only impression we can form of Solomon's Temple is from the detailed description in *I Kings 6*. It was a rectangular building running east and west, with a portico at the east end, a nave flanked by small rooms three storeys high and at the west end a holy of holies in which the Ark stood in dim mystery guarded by winged cherubim. In front of the building stood the Altar of Sacrifice, and it has been suggested[19] that this stood on the highest point of the rock, which is now crowned by the Dome of the Rock. Adjacent were other ceremonial features, the pillars Jachin and Boaz, the 'bronze sea', an enormous basin supported on twelve bronze oxen, and other mobile (though very massive) basins. Surrounding the whole were the inner and outer courts.

It is a significant fact that the Temple was only a part of a whole complex of buildings, for to the south of it was Solomon's palace, and it has been claimed that the Temple was essentially a chapel attached to the king's residence. In a mere fifty years, David and Solomon had created an authoritarian monarchy that was far from the loose tribal organization of the early days of settlement, with which was associated a deity whose abode was as temporary as that of his people.

The key to the appearance of the Temple is given by the fact that Solomon sent to Hiram, King of Tyre, not only for the materials, especially for the great timbers of cedar from which both the interior of the Temple and the forty-five pillars of the hypostyle hall in his palace, called the House of the Forest of Lebanon, were constructed, but also for the craftsmen to work the timbers and the stone. All the archaeological evidence from Palestine goes to show that the Israelites themselves lacked any skill as masons and craftsmen. Evidence of the skill of the Phoenicians in working stone from the second millennium onwards comes from sites such as Ras Shamra and Byblos and from the remains of Tyre itself, though most of the latter have to be studied below the waters of the Mediterranean. Evidence of their skill as craftsmen in ivory and bronze comes from a wide area stretching from North Syria to Cyprus. Still more revealing in relation to Jerusalem is the evidence from Samaria. Here, some eighty years later (*c.* 880 BC), Omri, ruler of the Northern Kingdom of Israel, built himself a new capital. Omri's contacts with Phoenicians are shown by the marriage of his son Ahab to the Phoenician princess Jezebel. Excavation has shown[20] that the masonry of the buildings of Omri and Ahab is Phoenician. The masonry is truly exquisite, the heavy walls bold and forceful, the interior walls with stones dressed to a beautifully tooled smooth face and fitted together with minute precision. We can imagine that the walls of Solomon's Temple and palace were of the same fine masonry, and that the platform was constructed of stones with the bolder type of dressing. Though so much of this has to be deduced from the mere statement that Phoenician masons were employed in the work, one link in architectural style can be based on the evidence of the excavations. Against the foot of the summit scarp on the eastern side (immediately east of Site P in Fig. 6) excavations disclosed a tumble of ashlar blocks with the fine, smooth faces of Omri's building at Samaria, and amongst them two halves of a pilaster capital of Proto-Ionic type. This is precisely the type of capital found at Samaria and at other sites that have architectural links with Samaria. This tumble of masonry, obviously from an important building which had stood on top of the scarp, may be the one architectural relic of Solomon's Jerusalem so far found.

Plates 18, 19

Plate 20

From Samaria again, and from the wider Phoenician world, we may draw further deductions as to the appearance of the Temple. Its form, the tripartite sequence culminating in an inner sanctuary, has a long history in Semitic lands. In Palestine as early as the third

Plates 22, 23

millennium, in the Early Bronze Age, a similar arrangment has been claimed for a sanctuary at 'Ai[21]. A most interesting Canaanite temple at Hazor existed throughout much of the second half of the second millennium[22], which in its turn closely resembles a temple of the thirteenth century BC at Atchana in northern Syria[23]. The ninth century BC temple at Tell Tainat[24] provides a good Phoenician parallel which is nearly contemporary. When Yahweh was thus given a permanent abode, it was of a type traditional in Semitic religions.

The mere fact of a permanent abode for the god of the Israelites, who were still looking back to the austerities of nomadic life with pride, is revolutionary enough. Still more so are its furnishings and adjuncts. The strangely ornamented columns Jachin and Boaz, the elaborate bronze bowls, the cherubim, those winged figures with the body of a lion and human heads, the luxuriant use of gold, all has a most exotic and heavily ornate sound. Obviously, no contemporary buildings have survived to a sufficient extent to provide us with full archaeological parallels, but archaeological discoveries in recent years have shown us enough of the culture of the contemporary Syrian world to illustrate individual objects, and to show how completely at home Solomon's Temple was in its surroundings. The thirteenth century BC temple at Hazor already mentioned was provided with an elaborate equipment of bowls, lavers, altars and offertory tables, and its door was defended by massive lion orthostats[25]. The Late Bronze Age Temples at Lachish had again a most elaborate ceremonial equipment[26]. Finds of bronze vessels from Cyprus show, though on a much smaller scale, what the lavers mounted on wheels must have looked like[27]. But again perhaps Samaria provides the example nearest in time and place to the general style of decoration. In the area of the palace of Omri and Ahab were found many fragments of the ivory carvings, mainly plaques, but some carved in the round, which had decorated the furniture and perhaps the walls. It was recognized at the time of the excavations[28] that these ivories were

Plate 23
Plate 21

Plate 24

Plate 27

Phoenician, a product of the Phoenician eclectic art, exquisite in execution but not original in inspiration, drawing instead on the art of Egypt and Mesopotamia for style and tradition. Since the date of these excavations, the wealth of Syria in such work has been abundantly illustrated by the finds at Nimrud in Assyria[29]. Neither Samaria nor the much greater wealth of Nimrud can show to the archaeologist walls or floors overlaid with gold; if gold had been used in such a way, the depredations of robbers would have long ago removed such tempting booty. But even the poor surviving fragments at Samaria shows evidence of the lavish use of gold on the carvings, and at Nimrud whole panels were certainly originally gold coated[30]. Neither at Samaria nor Nimrud do cherubim 10 cubits (5 metres) high[31] survive, but one has only to magnify in one's imagination plaques such as those from Samaria[32] and Nimrud[33] to visualize these strange creatures brooding over the Ark in the twilight of the Holy of Holies.

Solomon's Temple thus introduced into Jerusalem, and into the midst of the Israelites, the full luxury of the current Syro-Phoenician culture. The adjacent palace was no doubt equally luxurious and worthy of an oriental potentate, a ruler of an important state to which the conquests of David had for a short time elevated Israel. Excavations at Jerusalem have so far failed to provide evidence of the extent to which the rest of the capital was beautified, and, as has been explained in connection with David's city, may never be able to do so. The find of the fallen stones and pilaster capital already mentioned (p. 59) suggests that there may have been at least a few buildings outside the palace and Temple area that had some architectural pretensions. On general grounds one may feel some doubt as to the extent to which non-official buildings benefited from the standards of luxury and beauty applied to the buildings belonging to the king. The taxing of the people, or the demand for forced labour, required for the royal buildings clearly imposed a heavy burden, and

Plates 25, 26

Plate 25

Plates 25–27

resentment against this had a part in the causes of the break up of the united monarchy. Solomon certainly carried out public works in other important cities, for the tax to build the Temple was imposed also for buildings at Megiddo, Hazor and Gezer[34]. Town walls at these sites attributable to Solomon have been identified[35]. So far, there is not much evidence concerning the buildings within these town walls; what there is suggests nothing very grand[36]. Certainly there is nothing to suggest that the houses of the mass of the population emulated the style of the official buildings. The whole evidence suggests that, in contemporary towns and villages which did not enjoy the benefit of royal interest, the indigenous traditions continued and the way-of-life remained simple and unpretentious. Certainly at Samaria it is clear that when the dynasty of Omri ended, the native building methods returned; the Phoenician craftsmen were not assimilated and did not teach a succeeding generation of Israelites. One may therefore suspect that only the official parts of Jerusalem were changed, and that the rest continued much as before.

Plate 28

Plate 19

The Divided Monarchy:

Jerusalem as the Capital of Judah

THE SEPARATE DEVELOPMENT of the southern tribes and the northern tribes in the period of the Judges, with Jerusalem as the focal physical point in enemy hands rendering difficult the contact between the two, was undoubtedly a basic factor in the break-up of the United Monarchy of David and Solomon into the separate and antagonistic kingdoms of Judah and Israel. The United Monarchy had a brief life of some seventy years. About 930 BC the northern tribes broke away, to form the separate kingdom of Israel. Jerusalem was left to be the capital of the southern kingdom of Judah. Judah, small in area, and encircled by potentially and often actually hostile states, became the junior and poorer relation, though the status of Jerusalem as the site of the Temple made it in the event the centre of Jewish national aspirations.

The history of Jerusalem during the period of the divided monarchy is illustrated by only sparse archaeological evidence. The limits of the town remained basically the same, and the terraces on the eastern slope were maintained in repair as an essential element in the plan of the town. But the same reasons that have prevented us from obtaining any evidence concerning the interior buildings of the Davidic and Solomonic periods affect also the succeeding period.

Plates 29, 30

The best evidence concerning the ninth-eighth centuries comes in fact from outside the contemporary town wall. After the identification of the position of the early wall at the east end of the main trench on the eastern slope, an effort was made to pick up its line in the area marked A XXI–XXII on the plan. The wall was not found, as it was

Fig. 6

Plate 31

subsequently shown to have run rather more obliquely. What was found, however, was very interesting. The first feature to emerge was a shallow cave in the face of a rock scarp. Against its lower, eastern, side, three substantial walls formed an enclosure, leaving a gap *c.* 1.15 metres by 0.60 metres against the face of the rock. The walls were continued to form small rooms, but the importance of the enclosure outside the cave was emphasized by the fact that the walls and the enclosure had been carefully covered with mud-plaster, which had been cut into once and then re-plastered. This filling of the mouth of the cave and then re-opening prompted the first interpretation of the complex as a tomb. At Jericho, tombs were rock-cut chambers approached by rock-cut shafts. The rock surface at Jericho was however more or less level, and the much steeper slope at Jerusalem would render approach by a rock-cut shaft impossible. First appearances suggested that the enclosing walls were a substitute for the shaft.

Plates 32, XVII

The first finds seemed to fit this hypothesis well. At the base of the enclosure wall was a large fill of intact pottery vessels. At Jerusalem, as on most town sites, the finding of an intact vessel is a rare event. On the other hand, in tombs there is a much greater chance that pottery vessels, placed there as part of the offerings to the dead, will survive intact. Moreover, when a tomb is used for a number of successive interments, the offerings placed with earlier individuals are often pushed out of the tomb and piled in the shaft. This was exactly the appearance that this pile suggested. But the completion of the excavation of the cave showed that it was not a tomb, for burials were entirely lacking. It cannot be argued that the bones have completely decayed away, for there are plenty of examples of preserved bones to show that the soil of Jerusalem does not have this effect. It must be accepted that the cave was not a tomb.

It could remain that the feature was a cenotaph, a memorial to someone, or a tomb prepared for him, who had died elsewhere and whose body had not been brought back. But at this stage it had become clear that the whole of the structure must be cleared before it could be interpreted. This process is not yet complete, but it is already apparent that we are concerned with a sanctuary or cult centre.

The first extension of the excavation showed that immediately to the north of the cave complex, and on the same level as it, was a small room in which there were two monolithic pillars. They are not roof supports, as the room was too small to require this. They must be interpreted as cult stones or *mazzeboth*. Such stones could be erected as a memorial, such as Jacob erected over the grave of Rachel, or as he erected at Bethel to commemorate his dream. But much the most common use was as cult symbols at a sanctuary, often near an altar. Because of the association of such *mazzeboth* with Canaanite cults they were condemned as pagan by the Israelite prophets.

As clearance in the area continued, further features emerged to support the identification of the complex as a cult centre. On the rock surface above the scarp in which the cave was hollowed was a small stone-built structure, isolated and much too small to be a room. The most probable interpretation is that it was the base of an altar. A more puzzling feature was a blocked doorway. This was in the west wall of the *mazzeboth* room. This wall was built almost up against the scarp in which the cave was hollowed. In fact, when the blocking was removed, one could lean through, but not go through. It could be that libations had to be poured here, but it remains obscure what the libations were honouring, for the removal of the wall showed only that it stood on an enormous boulder, and the removal of the boulder showed only solid rock behind it.

The complex extends still further to the north beyond the area so far cleared. The completion of the work here may add other features. But it is already very probable that we have an altar, cult stones, and evidence of some ritual that remains obscure; into this

Plate 35

Plates 33, 34

picture the original cave fits as a *favissa*, a depository for discarded vessels that had been offered to a diety and could not thereafter pass into profane use.

The pottery suggests a date of *c*. 800 BC. The Biblical record shows that there is no reason to be surprised at finding a shrine of an unorthodox cult even at Jerusalem, for the prophets were forced continually to inveigh against the backslidings of both king and people. The Biblical evidence suggests that sanctuaries of Baal were to be found in Jerusalem under the reigns of all three kings, Joash[37], Amaziah[38] and Azariah[39], whose rule covers the period *c*. 835–739 BC. The place for the sanctuary of an unorthodox cult was customarily outside the walls. Solomon's Temple of Baal was probably on the Mount of Olives. The provisional conclusion therefore is we have here, outside the eastern wall of the city, the sanctuary of an unorthodox cult, in use in the central period of the Divided Monarchy.

There was little peace for Judah during this period. When she was not at war with Israel to the north, she was often at war with her neighbours further south, especially from the east, where Ammon, Moab and Edom were perpetual menaces. The repair of the defences, after each of those numerous times in which it is recorded that Jerusalem was captured, was an urgent task, especially on the east side where the whole structure of the town depended on the soundness of the supporting walls down the slope. After about a thousand years of life, the original defences were apparently so badly destroyed that they were superseded by a new wall. This may have been as late as the beginning of the seventh century BC, but the full assessment of the pottery and other evidence has not yet been made. It cannot have been much earlier than that date, yet in the succeeding century or so there were no less than six rebuilds.

The first of these may give the key to this rapid succession. It has disappeared with the utmost completeness in the area excavated. Its existence can however be deduced from a considerable succession of levels which overlie the original wall but are cut by a later one, which we may call Wall 3. The levels are horizontal and they consist of domestic installations, above which is a cobbled road surface; on this surface are layers of water-laid silt, which is cut by gullies, in turn filled by silt. On a slope such as that of this area, horizontal levels can only exist if further down the hill there was a massive wall to retain them. From this we can infer the existence of Wall 2, though not a stone of it survives.

Plate 37

A massive length of Wall 3 survives. Its history is, however, complex. As already said, it cut the levels contemporary with Wall 2, and the massive construction of its lower courses can be seen in Plate 38. The next event however was its collapse to ground level with the resulting debris. Two further collapses and rebuildings are shown by the stratification against its face, making Walls 4 and 5, and a yet further phase has, like Wall 2, completely vanished; its existence is proved by the fact that the successor on the line of Wall 5 was a house-wall, from which the stub of a floor projected to the east, to be cut by the denudation lines. One can therefore deduce that Wall 6 lay to the east, and has been completely destroyed.

Plates 36–38

Plate 38

The present dating evidence is clear. The whole sequence lies within the period ± 700 BC, down to the final Babylonian destruction in 586 BC. Detailed work on the pottery remains to be done for the whole evidence to be accumulated (and work in a number of areas is still in progress). It is however improbable that in the present state of knowledge the niceties of pottery classification will enable any one stratum to be dated within a close term of years, and therefore enable any one destruction or rebuilding to be ascribed to a particular reign. It may be possible to ascribe a destruction to a known historical event, but this will be on probability only. The time when our predecessors ascribed work with certainty to the time of Solomon, Manesseh and so on, belongs to a past epoch. What again adds uncertainty to the ascription of an archaeologically proved destruction is that the forces of nature enter also into the problem. The detailed evidence of the present expedition has come mainly from the eastern slope, where the terraces, established by the Jebusites and maintained by David and his successors, were vulnerable not only to human destruction but to the destructions of earthquakes and torrential rains. The new walls described in the preceding paragraphs, from Wall 2 onwards were less well founded than their predecessor, built on bed-rock, and had an increasing pressure from the growing up-hill deposits. They therefore collapsed in rapid succession and this may have been for natural reasons or by human agency.

There is an event in the history of Jerusalem which is of vital historical importance, and for which there is dramatic archaeological evidence, though we are not yet ready to interpret it in the terms of the stratigraphy of the sites excavated. This is the saving of Jerusalem from the Assyrians in the time of Hezekiah, *c.* 700 BC. Previous references to the enemies of Judah have been concerned with their neighbours, comparatively petty powers. In the period of the establishment of the Hebrew monarchy in Palestine there was in neither Egypt nor Mesopotamia any strong central power. But in the eighth century BC, Assyria enters the picture. Its progress was not steady; dynastic struggles followed the death of each king. But each wave of expansion to the west spread further than its predecessor. In 722–720 BC, Samaria, capital of the Northern Kingdom, fell and its inhabitants were taken away into exile. One of the sporadic recessions followed, but by *c.* 700 BC a new advance threatened Jerusalem. Hezekiah, who ruled Judah from 720 to 685 BC, took steps that saved his capital, though Lachish, to the south-west, was captured, and much of Judah was devastated. Hezekiah's steps were partly those of diplomacy, in the attempt to buy off the Assyrians. A plague that struck the Assyrians may have helped in halting the attack. For these, no archaeological evidence can be expected. What archaeology can be expected to show is evidence of the steps Hezekiah took to strengthen the defences.

It is highly probable that these measures included repairs to the town wall. One among the successive walls on the eastern side, designated Walls 2 to 6 in the preceding paragraphs, almost certainly belongs to this time. It remains to be seen whether the full study of the finds will provide sufficiently precise evidence to prove that any one of them belongs to the time of Hezekiah.

For one of Hezekiah's measures, Biblical evidence and exploration combine to provide wholly satisfying evidence. The Bible tells us[40] that Hezekiah took steps to deny access to the water supply to the enemy and to secure it to the defenders. This certainly refers to the spring Gihon, of which the importance to Jerusalem has been already emphasized (pp. 15–16). After the Israelite conquest of Jerusalem, the overflow from the spring had apparently been conducted in a channel along the flank of the ridge to irrigate the 'king's garden'[41]. Whether the war-time access to the spring by shaft and tunnel (p. 22) was maintained, we do not know. Hezekiah apparently decided to conceal the source of the spring (this can be inferred from the phrase, 'he planned . . . to stop the water of the springs that were outside the city . . . saying 'Why should the Kings of Assyria come and find much water,'"[42]) and to conduct the waters to a point to which access from within the walls was both easy and safe. His great engineering operation for this purpose was the Siloam tunnel, through which the waters from the spring still flow into the Pool of Siloam in the central valley.

Plates 39, 40, VII

The tunnel follows a complicated course. First it runs back into the rocky flank of the ridge. It then turns south and follows the flank until it turns across the tip of the ridge to run into the pool in the central valley. As the plan shows, the course is sinuous. To many of those who have studied the problem, this sinuosity has demanded an explanation; for instance, that the excavators of the tunnel tried to avoid the area in which, many feet above, it has been suggested that the royal tombs were situated. Personally, I do not find this convincing.

Fig. 3

I do not believe there is any reason to suppose that the rock cuttings found by Weill[43] were the royal tombs, nor do I believe that even if they were, the tunnellers some 20 metres below the surface would have been either sufficiently aware of their position or, if they had been, have felt that they must avoid the sacred spot so far above them, by adding enormously to their labours in making the great detours. I believe that they ploughed ahead like moles, with a general sense of direction that might go astray and have to be corrected. It is less surprising that there were deviations than that the two sets of tunnellers, with no magnetic compasses or other modern aids, working from either end, ever met. The triumph of the meeting is recorded in the

Plate 41

Siloam Inscription found in 1880 in which it is said, 'This is the story of the boring through: whilst [the tunnellers lifted] the pick each towards his fellow and whilst three cubits [yet remained] to be bored [through, there was heard] the voice of a man calling his fellow, for there was a split in the rock on the right hand and on [the left hand]. And on the day of the boring through, the tunnellers struck, each in the direction of his fellows, pick against pick. And the water started to flow from the source to the pool, twelve hundred cubits. A hundred cubits was the height of the rock above the head of the tunnellers.'

Hezekiah's tunnel therefore brought the waters from the spring Gihon in the Kedron, the eastern valley, into the central valley, where

Plate 42

there is the present-day Pool of Siloam. For this course, there can be no query; one can follow it, and there is no possibility, with its rock-cut walls, of any deviation. With the plan of ancient Jerusalem as accepted before the excavations beginning in 1961, this fitted excellently. In the plan produced by the excavation of the 1890's the central valley and the flanking western ridge are shown within the area of Jerusalem in the period of Hezekiah. But the latest excavations have shown conclusively that the western ridge, or at least its southern end, was not incorporated into the city until the first century AD.

This means that if we now assert that the western ridge was outside the city, one must explain why, when Hezekiah was assuring the water-supply from the spring Gihon to the inhabitants of Jerusalem, he could do so by bringing the water to the present position of the Pool of Siloam in the central valley. Looked at today, this seems extremely difficult. The central valley is narrow at this point and the western ridge rises steeply. Any wall swinging out from the tip of the eastern ridge to enclose the Pool would have lain at the foot of the western ridge in a militarily impossible position, for it could never have been carried high enough to prevent it being overlooked at very close range by attackers on the western ridge. However, to test even such an improbable site a trench was dug at Site O and it was clear that there had never been a wall at this spot.

Plate 44

The explanation, and one that seems to me completely satisfactory, came not from excavation but from observation. The present south-west tip of the eastern ridge is cut by an artifical scarp and at the base of the vertical cut is an overhang. Beneath this today runs the water flowing out of the Pool. As one looks at the scarp and the overhang, it is quite clear that the scarp has cut away the outer side of a rock-cut channel and made it open to the air. The waters from the spring Gihon were therefore carried to the reservoir in the central valley in a rock-cut channel, and the overflow continued to the south in another enclosed channel along the western flank of the eastern ridge. Today this looks incomprehensible, for it would be much simpler to allow the water to run down the centre of the valley. The only reasonable explanation is that the reservoir was itself rock-covered, in fact a cistern rather than an open pool, and that to conceal its position, the overflow was continued a distance of some 100 metres, only to become visible on the surface, perhaps disguised by filtering out through a pile of rocks, well down the slope of the Kedron Valley. If one once accepts that the reservoir was a roofed cistern, completely cut in the rock, all the difficulties disappear. There is no longer any need for the

Plate 43
Plate VIII

I   The Dome of the Rock, seen from across the Valley of the Kedron, with the walls of Suleiman the Magnificent in the foreground

II   The eastern slope of the eastern ridge, the site of the original city. The spring Gihon, or the Virgin's Fountain, which provided the water supply vital to the city, lies under the lower of the two small buildings in the centre (pp. 15–16)

III   The slope of the eastern ridge down to the Kedron valley, seen from the north-east (p. 24)

IV   The terraces constructed in the fourteenth-thirteenth centuries BC to provide a foundation for houses above the steeply-sloping rock slope. At the base, earlier walls, dating back to the original town of the eighteenth century BC. The man at the top is on the floor of a house of the seventh century BC (pp. 32, 49)

V   The trench down the eastern slope laid out in squares at an early stage in the excavations (pp. 23–4)

VI   The trench down the eastern slope, as extended in 1962, showing how the stony tumble distorted the original layout (pp. 24, 107–9)

VII   The northern end of the Siloam Tunnel, with the roof only *c.* 1.75 metres high (pp. 69–70)

VIII   The scarp which truncates the tip of the eastern ridge and has cut away the side of the channel carrying the overflow from the Pool of Siloam (pp. 71–77)

IX   Herodian masonry of the Wailing Wall, on the west side of the Temple platform (p. 142)

X   The great depth of fill in Site C. The figures in the foreground stand on bedrock. The figure half-way up stands beside the drain incorporated in the fill (pp. 151–3)

I

II

V

IV

III

VI

VII VIII

IX X

 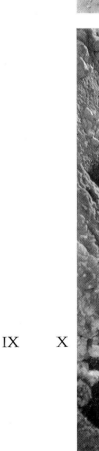 

reservoir to be within the walls. All that had to be defended was the access to it, probably by steps in a gallery or by a shaft.

Ultimately the roof of the cistern must have collapsed. All evidence concerning this has disappeared in the present structure of the Pool, in origin possibly Roman, and in the Byzantine church which lies above it[44]. The line of the defences probably disappeared at the same time. It is possible that a portion of it survives above the vertical scarp, but the dating evidence, which on masonry evidence alone could belong to almost any period from the tenth to the second centuries BC, has been removed in previous excavations.

V

The Last Century of Royal Jerusalem

HEZEKIAH'S EFFORTS saved Jerusalem in the immediate crisis. Internal events in Assyria, and the beginnings of a resurgence of Egyptian power, reduced pressure on the small powers of the Mediterranean coast. Judah thus maintained a nominal and precarious independence for another hundred years.

In terms of material remains, this century bulks large, for to it belongs an enormous proportion of the finds of Iron Age date, pottery, figurines, weights, stone utensils, bone objects. The reason for this is one of those apparent anomolies in archaeology. A period that ends in a great destruction usually yields a wealth of objects. The debris of collapse covers the houses and their contents, which the inhabitants had no time to salvage, and a great depth of destruction debris protects them from subsequent disturbance. The disastrous destruction of Jerusalem by the Babylonians in 586 BC, provided just such a setting for the recovery of remains of the preceding period.

Even given such conditions favourable to archaeological evidence, the area of Jerusalem in which this is available is limited. The longer the excavations continue, the more apparent it becomes that on the summit archaeological evidence has been completely destroyed. Earlier excavations have contributed something to this, but in most areas quarrying in the Roman period had already been all-destructive.

The evidence for structures of the seventh century BC, comes almost entirely from the eastern slopes. On the lower part of the slopes, the importance of the platforms and substructures supporting the main buildings is once more emphasized. The repairs to the original platforms here were very massive. In the area of the main trench down

Plate 45

the slope, a substructure of massive blocks went right down to bedrock, and the highest surviving portion consisted only in the base of a cistern, so the actual buildings were probably at least three metres higher. Lower down the slope there were rooms, but again the walls were so massive that they clearly supported structures at a higher level. These massive walls continued down the slope to join the succession of town walls, Walls 3 to 6, which have already been described, but evidence does not survive to ascribe them to any one stage in the succession of town walls.

It is only at the summit of the slope that what one might call the surface buildings, as distinct from the substructures, actually survive. Here, the area excavated was expanded beyond the 11 metre width of Trench I. This area excavated had a basic difference from north to south. To the north, beneath the seventh century levels, the imme-diately succeeding fill belonged to the Late Bronze Age, Jebusite, terrace, built up against a retaining wall to the east with a stone fill divided into compartments by single-course facing walls. A succession of repairs had been carried out to this system of compartmental fills, repairing a succession of collapses to the south. These, it is suggested above, originated in the repairs of David and Solomon to *Millo*. At any rate, the repairs to the platform structure continued right down to the seventh century BC. The excavation of these structures was in fact a horrible problem. The Israelite builders who added to the original fill employed very massive stones. They were mostly quite unworked. Many looked as if they were *wadi* boulders, which must therefore been brought up from the valley some 100 metres away and 40 metres lower down. But even if they had been quarried from the fairly immediate vicinity, to raise them into position in the wall must have involved an incredible amount of labour and of engineering skill. Our problem was simply to penetrate down into the structures to establish their nature and date. We could therefore break up the huge stones into manageable dimensions. Even so, these structures

Plates 29, IV

Plates 29, 30

were a colossal problem. As we worked downwards, the area had gradually to be contracted, for, as each course in the fill was reached, more and more stones projected into the area being dug that could not be moved without causing a collapse in the overlying courses. Eventually, the area narrowed to nothing, and we were unable to reach the base without starting again right from the top, a task which was too daunting to undertake in view of the probability that it would add nothing significant to our understanding of the structures. At that stage, we were, to judge from the area just to the north, some 2 metres above bedrock, or about 0.50 metres above the base of the original platforms.

Plate 13

As just mentioned, in this area to the north the original basic structure of the Late Bronze Age terraces survived and it could be seen how these had collapsed in a southerly direction. The reason for this southerly collapse is an interesting problem. One would have expected that the main pressure from the massive fill would have been down the slope to the east. Collapses down this slope could indeed be traced, but in this area they were not as serious as the collapses to the south. It is possible that there was a line of weakness here due to the fill of a natural hollow. It is more tempting, however, to conjecture that there was here a retaining wall dividing the terraces from a lower area to the south, and to conjecture that this lower area was to provide a route to the summit from a water-gate leading to the spring. To prove this would mean an even more demanding excavation than that we carried out, for here the overlying levels had not been removed by the previous excavators and indeed on them they had piled up their dumps. We therefore have had to leave this in the realm of conjecture, with perhaps the suggestion that it might be an area of interest to future excavators, always provided that by this time the whole area has not been built over.

Whatever the cause, in the area to the north of that in which there were the Iron Age repairs, the Late Bronze Age terraces had survived.

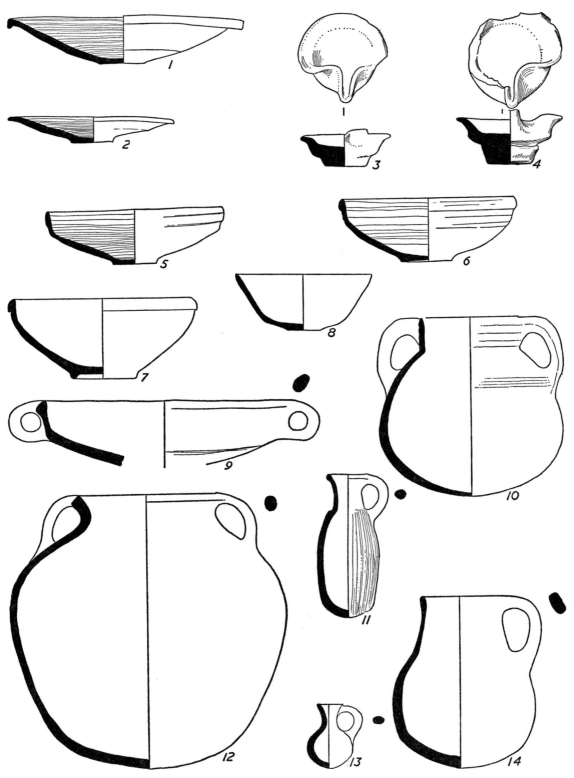

7 *A selection of typical pottery vessels of the seventh century BC*

Plate 46

Directly on top of the compartmented stone filling were the floors of the Iron Age houses. Not a single trace remained of the original houses which must have stood here, and not even their level is certain, for the Iron Ages houses were themselves terraced into the original filling. These houses extend also over the Iron Age repairs to the terraces to the south, but here they were less well preserved. There was a succession of floors, which could be associated with alterations or additions to the buildings. But all seem, on a provisional analysis of the pottery, to belong to the seventh century BC. This was certainly the date of the final stage, for which the plan of the buildings could best be established.

Plates 47, 48

The buildings are not in themselves impressive. Most of the rooms are small, and the walls are dry-built of roughly shaped stones, with little attempt at coursing. When the houses were in use, the superficial appearance of the walls would not have been quite so rough, for they were faced with mud plaster. Nevertheless, the builders had returned to the ancient Palestinian methods; the excellent building-techniques of the Phoenician masons imported by Solomon were entirely lost when Hiram's technicians returned home. The evidence at Samaria

Plate 19

was similar. When the Phoenician masons imported by Omri and Ahab departed, the locals showed no skill at all in copying them, and reverted to the age-old rough masonry of the land.

Plates 47, 48

As has been said, the rooms were small and irregularly planned. They were built in terraces cut into the underlying platforms. Evidence for this is a staircase, a secondary structure inserted into an earlier room. The staircase must have led to a higher Iron Age level above them, but the overlying fill was inserted in the second-first centuries BC to support a weak area at this point, and it was impossible to explore the underlying levels without endangering the Maccabean town wall on the summit.

Plate 50

The general plan is close to that of many sites of the period in the hill-country of Judah. In one room was a typical oven, a clay dome

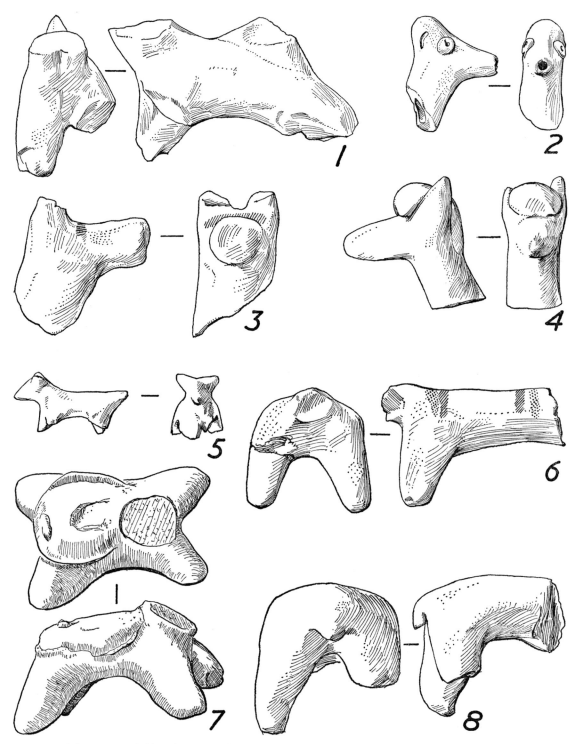

8   Animal figurines, probably cult objects, of the seventh century BC

Plates 49, 53

set on the floor, which is clear evidence that the structures were domestic. Another room entirely typical of Iron Age II in Palestine survives in part at the north end of the area excavated. This was on a plan for the larger rooms of the period found at many places; the best examples perhaps come from Tell en Nasbeh, some eight miles north of Jerusalem. The standard plan is a hall divided into a central nave and two side aisles by lines of monoliths which presumably supported the roof. The place where the eastern line of monoliths should come is just where erosion, clearly visible, has carried away

Plate 53

the whole side of the building. Even though this room was presumably the principal room of the house, the walls were of the same rough masonry.

This is the only group of rooms so far found that can be safely ascribed to Jerusalem in Old Testament times. More important buildings may have existed on the summit of the ridge, but the improbability that any evidence of them will be recovered has already been stressed. The evidence from Samaria, however, suggests that even if these buildings were more spacious and solid, in actual structure any that were built after the departure of Solomon's Phoenician masons would have been in the same rough masonry.

In the ruins of these houses and of the structures down the slope were found a great number of examples of the household equipment typical of the seventh century BC. An overwhelming preponderence of the finds consisted of potsherds, fragments of the vessels which were crushed in the destruction of the buildings and scattered in the

Fig. 7

subsequent process of erosion. Examples of this pottery are very common, so one tends to despise them. But it is in fact some of the most attractive pottery in the whole history of Palestinian ceramics. The numerous examples of a comparatively limited range of forms, made on the wheel, does suggest mechanization. The attractiveness lies in the finish. Bowls, dishes, jugs and juglets are finished with a surface slip, in most cases a darkish red, sometimes buff or yellowish,

25 When Solomon set about building a temple worthy to house the Ark of the Covenant, he called upon Hiram, King of Tyre, to send masons and craftsmen as well as to supply the cedarwood to be employed in the building. In building such a temple, Solomon was emulating his contemporaries in Syria, and from the evidence that has survived to us from Western Asia we can give substance to the Biblical descriptions. The illustration here shown is of one of the ivories found at Nimrud in Assyria, where the rulers accumulated vast collections of *objets d'art* from North Syria. In style it is a combination of Egyptian and Phoenician motives, such as could well have been provided in Jerusalem by the Phoenician craftsmen employed by Solomon. The gold leaf with which part of the carving is still overlaid is an illustration of the statement that the carvings in Solomon's Temple were overlaid with gold (pp. 60–61)

26, 27   The most striking element in the description of the holy of holies in Solomon's Temple is that of the cherubim of olivewood, each ten cubits (c. 5 metres) high. Each wing of the cherubim was five cubits long; their wings touched in the centre and their outer wings touched the side walls; the figures were overlaid with gold. The impression of these great figures guarding the Ark is one of mystery and brooding power. An illustration of the kind of figure that the writer of the Book of Kings is trying to convey in words to us is provided by an ivory from Nimrud, *left*, though the height of these figures is only c. 8.4 cms as compared with the 5 metres of the figures in the holy of holies. At Samaria were also found ivory carvings, *right*. The Samaria carvings were mainly found in the debris of the Assyrian destruction in 722 BC. But there is little doubt that they belonged originally to the furnishings that caused the name 'house of ivory' to be given to Ahab's palace. They are thus local evidence of the influences of Phoenician art on Palestine

28   The great site of Megiddo was one of the cities in which Solomon carried out important building operations, for in *I Kings 9.15* it is stated that the levy that he raised was not only for his work in Jerusalem but also for work at Hazor, Megiddo and Gezer. Megiddo has a history much more ancient than that of Jerusalem, for its origins probably go back to the Neolithic period, and it was certainly an important site by at least the end of the fourth millennium BC. It also differs from Jerusalem in the fact that the majority of its structures were of mud-brick; the walls in their collapse gradually raised the level of the ground to create a *tell*, a man-made hill. By the time of Solomon this *tell* had assumed the imposing proportions shown in this view. A destruction at the end of the Canaanite stage had been followed by a period of abandonment. Solomon re-created it as a city, and the links between his fortifications there, which one would expect from the Biblical record, and those of Hazor and Gezer have been proved archaeologically (p. 62)

29, 30 The view, *opposite*, shows in the background the compartments of stone fillings that were constructed in the Late Bronze Age to provide the basis of buildings on the eastern slope of the ridge on which the original town of Jerusalem was situated, an area included within the defences not because it was attractive for buildings but because it was necessary to place the defences sufficiently low on the slope to protect access to the spring in the valley. The builders of the fourteenth–thirteenth century BC evolved this ingenious lay-out of terraces to enable full use to be made of the steep slope. The groundwork of these stone-filled terraces survived until the Babylonian destruction in 586 BC. But the vulnerability of a town founded on such an artificial base is shown by the fact that the only houses that survive destruction belong to the seventh century BC. Plate 13 illustrates the way in which these terraces had collapsed to the south. It is very probable that this was because beyond the area excavated there was a sunken approach from the spring to the summit, but this has not been proved. In the foreground, *opposite* and *above*, is a final rebuild of the original terraces using much more massive stones. The coursing is regular, but the stones themselves are irregular and undressed. The date is certainly Iron Age. It is very tempting to identify it with *Millo*. *Millo* was repaired by David and Solomon and various of their successors. The literal translation of the word is a filling. Here in this terrace structure we have something that is certainly a filling, and was vital to this part of Jerusalem (pp. 50–51, 63)

31, 32 So much of the superstructure of ancient Jerusalem has been destroyed that little of spectacular interest survives. An example is an area low on the eastern slope of the original site, which was outside the contemporary town walls. Against a rock scarp, above which the town wall had run, was a substantial structure enclosing the aperture of a shallow cave undercutting the scarp, as can be seen *above*. The aperture had been plastered over and reopened more than once. The first interpretation that suggested itself was that this was a tomb, cut in a rock slope too steep to have an approach by a shaft in the normal way, with, therefore, a shaft created by walls. This interpretation seemed to be supported by the find in the space between the walls and the rock of an accumulation of a great number of more or less complete pottery vessels. In tombs it is very usual that an accumulation of vessels is found in the shaft, displaced when later burials are made. But the tomb theory was disproved, since within the cave there was not the slightest suggestion of any burials (pp. 64–6)

33–35 Since the finds made in the area illustrated in Plates 31 and 32 were enigmatical the area of excavation was extended to the north. The first find was a room in which there were two monolithic piers shown in Plate 35; their relation to the view in Plate 31 is shown in Plate 34. In architecture of the Iron Age, monolithic piers are used on occasions as roof-supports. But here the area concerned is so small that roof-supports are not necessary. They are clearly standing-stones, *mazzeboth*, that is to say, Canaanite cult symbols which appear as heathen and abhorred elements in the Bible. A further extension of the excavated area showed that the *mazzeboth* room was bounded on the west side by a wall that was separated from the rock scarp by a distance of only *c.* 30 cms. Yet in this wall was a doorway, shown blocked as it was found in Plate 35, and in its original state in Plate 34. As Plate 33 shows, this doorway can have provided no real access; one could have lent through it but not walked through it. The clue may be given by the fact that on the surface of the scarp above was a rectangular stone structure, much too small to be a room; this is seen in Plates 33 and 34. It is probably to be interpreted as an altar; the doorway would have enabled libations to be poured in the space at the foot of the altar. The whole complex is probably to be interpreted as evidence of the unorthodox cults with sanctuaries outside the walls, for which the Bible provides ample evidence (pp. 64–6)

36–38 The archaeological evidence is clear that the original defences on the eastern side of the eastern ridge dated from *c.* 1800 BC and remained in use for about a thousand years. Plate 36 shows the first surviving wall to succeed these. The salient of the wall of 1800 BC (*see* Plates 10, 11) is seen disappearing beneath a very massive successor. Here its face stands 3.50 metres high, though, as Plates 37 and 38 show, it elsewhere stands 4.50 metres high. Its width is 5 metres, but since the rock is sloping up rapidly, the surviving portion is at the rear only a single course high, compared with the six courses of the face in Plate 36. But this wall was not in fact the first to succeed the original wall. In Plates 37 and 38 is seen a complex of structures that overlie the original wall. They include several sub-periods, and they are sealed by a road surface, which is cut into by a series of water channels. All of these demand an external wall to the east, for they have a horizontal base that can only have existed on such a slope if there was a retaining wall on the lower side. Therefore before the wall shown on these three views was built, there was one further to the east which has completely disappeared. The surviving wall shows evidence of a succession of building periods, and successive collapses against its base are shown in Plate 38. All these reconstructions date from the eighth to the sixth centuries BC, and are evidence of the dangers threatening Jerusalem at this time. The Biblical account shows how necessary it was for Jerusalem to be well defended, for on all sides there were nations with which Judah was at war from time to time, and from time to time Jerusalem suffered at the hands of these enemies. A more serious threat developed in the eighth century BC, when the imperial power of Assyria began steadily advancing to the west. In 722 BC, Samaria, capital of the kingdom of Israel was captured and destroyed, and in 700 BC, Jerusalem was threatened. It is to about this period that these rebuildings of the eastern defences belong, and one of the buildings or rebuildings was highly probably the work of Hezekiah in face of the Assyrian threat. When all the evidence has been assessed, it may be possible to say where in the sequence his wall comes (pp. 66–8)

39–42 The best known of Hezekiah's measures to defend Jerusalem against the Assyrians was to assure the water supply to the defenders and to deprive the enemy of access to it. The original shaft and tunnels, described on p. 22 had been to provide protected access from within the city, but the overflow from the spring had always run away down the Kedron. Hezekiah's scheme was much more radical. He diverted the whole flow of the spring into a tunnel that carried it through the hill to a reservoir on the western side; presumably access from the Kedron was simultaneously blocked. The tunnel runs back into the side of the ridge, then pursues a rather winding course along the eastern flank, to cross beneath the southern tip to the western side *(see Fig. 11)*. Various explanations have been suggested for the winding course, but the most probable is the difficulties the excavators of this rock-cut tunnel found in keeping to the correct line. The work was done by gangs working from each end. Near the far end an inscription (Plate 41) was found cut in the wall recording the joy of the two gangs when they at last met. Plate 40 shows the tunnel near the north end, Plate 39 near the south end, where it is very much higher. The probable explanation is that the gang at the south end misjudged the level and had to lower their floor very considerably to enable the water to flow. *Above*, the Pool of Siloam as seen today (pp. 69–71)

43, 44   The Siloam tunnel brought the water of the spring Gihon through the hill into the central valley, the Tyropoeon. The position of the present Pool of Siloam is seen in the view of the Tyropoeon from the south, *above*, where it lies just to the right of the minaret in the middle distance. The discovery in the 1961–7 excavations that the western ridge was not within the defences of Jerusalem until the first century AD, has created difficulties of interpretation, for it was the essence of Hezekiah's scheme that the new reservoir was covered by the defences. The present Pool lies outside these defences, in a position completely overlooked by the western ridge, which was accessible to the enemy, as can be seen in Plate 44. The explanation is provided by an examination of the rock at the southern end of the eastern ridge. As Plate 43 shows, the whole of the tip of the ridge has been cut away. At the base of this scarp is an overhang. Plate VIII shows that beneath this overhang runs the overflow from the Pool. Clearly, this once ran in a rock-cut channel, the outer side of which was removed by the scarp. The overflow would only have been carried through a tunnel if it was desired to conceal it, for it would have been much simpler to allow it to escape down the centre of the valley. This implies that the reservoir was also concealed, and was in fact a rock-cut cistern. Its position would then have been unknown to the enemy, and the overflow would have only emerged well away from it, down the slope of the Kedron. Access to it would have been provided from within the defences by a shaft or staircase. Presumably eventually the roof of the cistern collapsed, and it became the open pool that it is today. Its present state is shown in Plate 42. In Roman times its surround was rebuilt, and in the Byzantine period a church was constructed above it (p. 71)

45   Very little of the structures within the walls of Jerusalem has survived. On the eastern side of the eastern ridge, the surviving portions consist of the Iron Age rebuilding of the Jebusite terraces, part of which is seen in Plates 29 and 30. This view again shows how exceedingly massive they were. Nothing of the superstructure survives. The figure on the right is standing on the floor of a cistern. Very likely the substructures included many cisterns, as is customary in the East. The ground floor of the actual houses would therefore have been well above this level. The structures were in use down to the period of the Babylonian destruction in 586 BC. Above is the tumble of stones derived from the collapse of buildings higher up the slope (pp. 78–9)

sometimes black, especially in the case of juglets. This slip is highly burnished or polished, a process carried out on the wheel (except with portions of jugs or juglets where this was not possible) by pressing on the revolving vessel a shell, stone, or bone tool which flattened and polished the slip. The combination of the polished surface, with the character given to it by the individual lines of the polished implement, is most pleasing.

Innumerable examples were also found of utilitarian vessels, lamps (rather unpleasing and heavy), cooking pots and storage jars for all sorts of commodities; the latter, being large vessels, were usually so fragmentary that their complete form cannot be recovered.

Second only to the fragments of pottery vessels were the fragments of figurines, human and animal. It is always possible to say that an animal figurine has no greater significance than that of a toy. The human figurines, which are for the most part of the elemental mother-goddess type, are certainly fertility cult objects, and the probability is that all the figurines have the same significance. The mother-goddess type has a pillar-shaped lower part and hands clasped below the breasts. No complete examples have been found, but the heads have either a square-cut, wig-like coiffeur, or have pinched, bird-like features. The animals are very schematically moulded. Some look like dogs, while some were certainly horses, as there are traces of bridles and, in a few cases, of riders. Again none were even approximately complete. It is in fact remarkable that though literally hundreds of fragments have been found, there is not a single one that can even be mended into a complete object; it could even be conjectured that they were intentionally broken.

Objects of personal adornment were rare. There are a few bronze fibulae or brooches, of the usual type with an angular bow decorated with mouldings, and a few bronze earrings, with a bronze wire to pierce the lobe of the ear, and a bead-like ball attached to it. A few fragments could be interpreted as parts of bronze bangles, and there

Figs 8–10

9   Fertility figurines of the seventh century BC

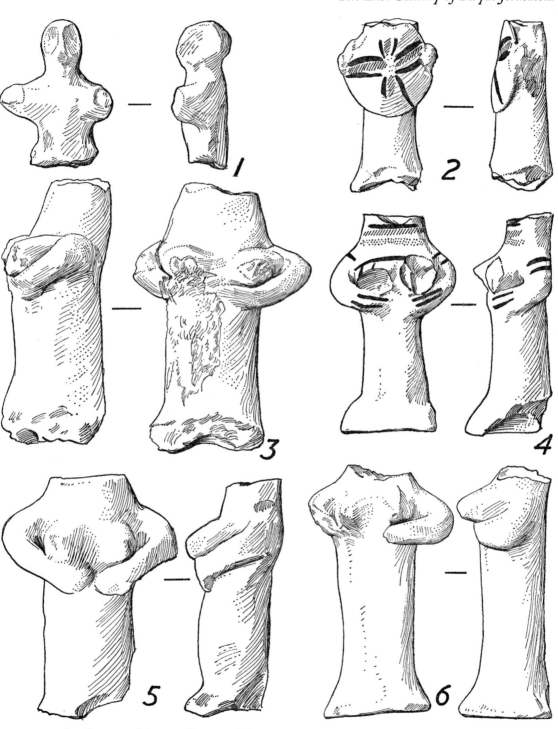

10   Fertility figurines of the seventh century BC

Plate 51

were also some fragments of bone pins. As far as the surviving evidence goes, the inhabitants of this part of Jerusalem were not a luxurious lot.

The most interesting find in these rooms was a large group of stone weights, many of them marked with their weight in shekels or, more rarely, *neseph* or *payim*. Before this find, these weights had been comparatively rare. The find of this group of forty one weights more than doubled the number known before, and more have been found in other parts of the site since. They range from $^1/_4$ *neseph* (2.57 grams) to 24 shekels (268.24 grams)[45]. Not only are they of scientific importance, they are attractive objects in themselves, polished to a beautiful finish, and usually of delicately tinted limestone.

Throughout the greater part of the seventh century BC the kings of Judah were vassals of Assyria. In 612 BC, the Assyrian Empire was destroyed by the Babylonians. For a short time an attempt was made by Egypt to rule Palestine and Syria, but in 605 BC, the Pharaoh Necho was defeated by Nebuchadnezzar at Carchemish. The Babylonians thereafter renewed the policy of Assyria of expansion towards the west. Johoiakim of Judah was tempted to rely on Egypt, but he misjudged the situation, and in 597 BC, Nebuchadnezzar captured Jerusalem. The king and some thousands of the chief inhabitants were carried into exile. Jerusalem was not however completely destroyed, and it is usually accepted that the plundering of the Temple was only partial. Zedekiah, a member of the royal house, was set up as king, in vassaldom to Babylon.

Zedekiah again was tempted into revolt by the hope of Egyptian support. After nine uneasy years, Judah was committed to rebellion against Babylon, and the might of Babylon descended upon her. Jerusalem withstood an eighteen months siege, but in 586 BC the walls were breached, the city captured and completely destroyed. Many of the leaders were put to death, and the king and all the population except the poorest in the land were carried away into captivity. This was the end of the kingdom of Judah.

VI

Post-Exilic Jerusalem

IN 586 BC JERUSALEM was left in ruins and deprived of its leading citizens. It ceased even to be the centre of government, which was transferred to Mizpah[46], probably Tell Nasbeh, some eight miles to the north. It was not, however, completely abandoned, for the poorest in the land were specifically left behind[47]. They, with others from outside the town, endeavoured to carry on worship in the Temple, and the exiles in Babylon from time to time were able to send them gifts to help them to do this. In the main, however, the succeeding fifty years is a Dark Age; literary evidence is lacking, and so far archaeology has not filled the gap. All that one can say is that Judah, and probably her eastern neighbours Ammon and Moab were incorporated in the provincial system of the Babylonian Empire. In a number of sites there are indications, such as buildings that appear to have an official character, of local centres of government. But there is no doubt that life and culture in Palestine was at a low ebb.

Judah experienced little but suffering from the Neo-Babylonian Empire. But the Neo-Babylonian control over western Asia was of short duration. In 539 BC Babylon was captured by Cyrus, and Achaemenid Persian control rapidly spread to the whole area of the Neo-Babylonian Empire. The policy of the Achaemenid rulers to subject races was more humane than that of the Babylonians. Permission was given to the Judaean exiles to return to their native land. By no means all of those whose families had been residents of Jerusalem were prepared to give up the comforts of a city in which they had been brought up for a return to the ruins of a city that had been the home of their ancestors. This struggle between present amenities and ancestral and religious loyalties was a basic problem in the re-establishment of Jewish life in Palestine.

With the permission of the Achaemenid rulers of Mesopotamia, the first group of exiles returned *c.* 539–8 BC. In Jerusalem they found a town that was ruinous, but, as has already been said, not abandoned. In the destruction of 586 BC, the attention of the attackers would have been concentrated on the defences and on vital public buildings such as the Temple. The effect of the destruction of the defences on the eastern side has already been stressed. Houses here would have disappeared. On the summit of the hill, they would have been easily reparable. In this area, one can presume, the 'poorest in the land' continued to live. The Temple, no doubt, was very thoroughly destroyed. But, however great the destruction of the magnificent buildings dating from the period of Solomon, something survived to receive, as already mentioned, the gifts of the exiles to the remaining inhabitants who were endeavouring to maintain the traditional ceremonies.

The first wave of repatriated exiles returned to rebuild their own houses and to rebuild the Temple. It is a very probable supposition that they would not have been allowed to do more; a fortified city of Jerusalem would have stretched too far the tolerance of the Persian rulers, and would have certainly had adverse reactions from neighbouring countries such as Samaria and Ammon. Indeed, the Biblical record shows in the ensuing years just such mistrust on the part of the sovereign power and of the neighbouring states[48]. The first major activity of the returned exiles was to rebuild the Temple, and this Zerubbabel had completed by *c.* 516 BC[49]. According to the Biblical account, it was on the lines of the Temple of Solomon, and built in the same way, with a combination of ashlar blocks and beams of cedar[50]. But, like its predecessor, it has completely disappeared, and there is no hope that archaeology will reveal its remains.

It was not until Nehemiah was sent as governor that the walls of Jerusalem were rebuilt. Nehemiah ruled Jerusalem from the twentieth to the thirty-second year of Artaxerxes. There is unfortunately nothing to show whether the king in question is Artaxerxes I or Artaxerxes III. The probability is that it is the former, and that therefore Nehemiah was Governor of Jerusalem from 445 to 433 BC. Nehemiah's approach was that of any good organizer faced with such a problem. He started with a survey of the existing state of affairs. Presumably because he wished to be alone, and not to be plagued by those with their own theories of what should be done, or whose private interests were involved, he made his survey by night. We can read his description in the Book of Nehemiah of his progress along the north and west walls of the city. "I went out by night by the Valley Gate to the Jackal's Well and the Dung Gate and I inspected the walls of Jerusalem which were broken down and its gates which had been destroyed by fire."[51] There has been much learned discussion about the localization of the landmarks. But all this has been based on the supposition that the walls of the ruined Pre-Exilic city enclosed both the eastern and western ridges. As has been shown, this was not the case, and the walls that Nehemiah had to inspect are those shown in Fig. 6 and not those in Fig. 2.

No portion of the walls and gates inspected by Nehemiah on the north and west sides has been discovered and it is unlikely that any portion survives unless there are some remains buried beneath the platform of Herod's Temple. It is with reference to the eastern side that archaeological evidence links with the written record. When Nehemiah had completed his survey of the western side and reached the 'King's Pool', certainly to be identified as the Pool of Siloam or the adjacent Birket el Hamra, he turned to go up the valley, that is to say, the Kedron. He then says 'but there was no room for the beast that was under me to pass'[52]. Our excavations on the eastern slopes have revealed the tumbled mass of stones that blocked the way

Plate VI

of Nehemiah's donkey. We also know why the ruins were so much worse on the east side than the west, for it was only here that the buildings were terraced down into the valley in such a way that damage to the walls would result in wholesale devastation. A breach in the city wall at the base would bring down the structures supported against its rear, and it would need only a few winters' rains for the chain of collapse to spread up to the summit and far to either side. This can be vividly seen in the gulleys cut by winter storms to-day. The archaeological evidence is clear. Not only have areas of the tumbled stones derived from the destroyed structures been exposed, but there is a complete break in occupation after the end of the seventh century BC. When Nehemiah gave up his survey of the eastern walls, and went back inside the city, he decided to abandon the part of the town that lies on the eastern slope and to make the boundary on the east the crest of the comparatively level summit, as it had always been on the west. This decision was all the more reasonable in that only a fraction of the original population had returned from exile, so a smaller city was quite adequate, and also it was no longer necessary to safeguard access to the spring on the eastern side, now that the water ran through Hezekiah's tunnel to the western side of the town.

The Book of Nehemiah records how he set the inhabitants to work on the walls, dividing them into groups and giving to each group a defined section of the circuit[53]. The description is so detailed that many efforts have been made to interpret it in terms of recognizable topography. But the recent excavations have shown that the extent of the immediately Post-Exilic Jerusalem is very different from what has hitherto been supposed. The emphatic evidence shows that it was confined to the eastern ridge, with the area of the original town limited to the summit of the ridge, and beyond it to the north the extension added by Solomon. There is still some uncertainty as to the date at which the northern end of the western ridge was included;

Plate 52

Fig. 11

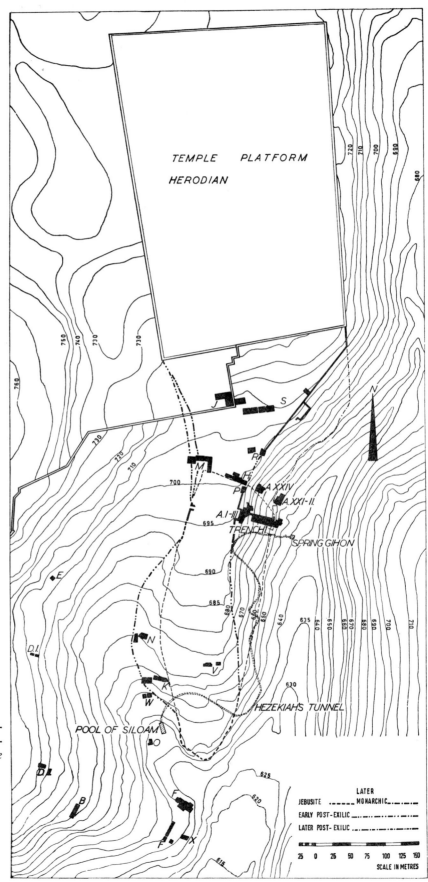

11 Plan of the walls of Jerusalem as restored by Nehemiah, with additions of the Maccabean period

TEMPLE PLATFORM
HERODIAN

SPRING GIHON

TRENCH

HEZEKIAH'S TUNNEL

POOL OF SILOAM

LATER
JEBUSITE - - - - - - MONARCHIC - · - · - · -
EARLY POST-EXILIC - - - · - - -
LATER POST-EXILIC - · · - · · - · ·

25   0   25   50   75   100   125   150
SCALE IN METRES

this is discussed below (p. 135). While the uncertainty remains, it is a waste of time to try to correlate the Biblical description of the line of Nehemiah's northern and western walls with the topographical features; even without that uncertainty much of the correlation would be guesswork. It is safer to concentrate on the factual archaeological evidence.

The salient point of Nehemiah's rebuilding of the walls is the rapidity with which it was accomplished. The triumphant conclusion was celebrated only fifty-two days after the work was put in hand[54]. If the plan of the Pre-Exilic city had been that hitherto accepted, as indicated in the plan of walls found in earlier excavations, the circuit of the walls involved would have been 4050 metres. The only possible explanation of the building of such a length of wall in fifty-two days would be that the earlier walls survived to a very substantial extent and that all that was required was the repair of breaches and short lengths, with perhaps particular concentration on the gateways. The new evidence shows that the circuit was probably only 2600 metres or, if the northern end of the western hill was included, at the most 4150 metres. It still remains reasonably certain from the Biblical record that much of the work was a repair of the eastern walls. The gang of 'Hanun and the inhabitants of Zanoah repaired the Valley Gate . . . as far as the Dung Gate. Malchijah . . . repaired the Dung Gate . . . And Shallum . . . repaired the Fountain Gate'[55]. This fits the archaeological evidence. Excavations on the slopes of the central valley (Sites K, N and M in the plan Fig. 11) show that the Pre-Exilic city was confined on this side to the summit, and that the first advance down the slopes came no earlier than the third–second century BC. In this area, enough of the earlier walls must have survived for the position of the gates to be recognizable and the walls to be capable of repair within in a relatively short period.

The state of affairs on the east side is recognizably different both on the archaeological evidence and in the Biblical account. In the latter, the gangs were set to work not from gate to gate, but from landmarks based on private property, from 'the door of the house of Eleashib to the end of the house of Eleashib . . . After them Benjamin and Hasshub repaired opposite their house'[56], and so on. The archaeological evidence shows dramatically that the artificial build-up of a town on the eastern slopes was abandoned, as has already been described. The old gates were far outside the new circuit. Nehemiah in his wall followed the eastern crest. In the area covered by the original Jebusite-Davidic city this line was, on present evidence, new. North of the north wall of the original city, it was however that followed by Solomon's extension. This had ceased to be a city wall with the northern extension on the slopes that took place in the eighth–seventh century[20a], but its line may still have been visible to be followed.

The archaeological evidence is not only clear that the eastern slope was abandoned, but has also enabled Nehemiah's wall to be identified. The excavations of 1923–6[57] uncovered a complex of walls on the summit, at the head of Trench I on the plan Fig. 11. Most of these proved to be of comparatively late date, *c.* second century BC, but the initial structure could be shown to be a substantial wall following the crest of the rock scarp bounding the summit. An excavation against the foot of this scarp showed that midden rubbish tipped over the wall, accumulating against the scarp, belonged to the fifth–fourth centuries BC. The wall could therefore be dated to the time of Nehemiah. It was solidly built, *c.* 2.75 metres thick, but its finish was rough, as might be expected in work executed so rapidly.

Plate 54

Plate 55

The line selected by Nehemiah continued to form the eastern boundary of the city until the original site was abandoned in Roman times, and was even re-used when the area was once more built up in the Byzantine period. On the west side, it can be taken that the line remained on the corresponding western scarp of the summit, here the original line, for wherever the problem has been tested by excavation, it can be shown that the first extensions only took place two hundred years or more later.

Jerusalem has in fact little written or archaeological history in the centuries following its restoration as a walled city. For the first century Judah remained part of the Persian Empire. The Persian rule was relatively benevolent and the Governor of Jerusalem, and other officials ruling in its name, were often apparently Jews. In various parts of the country, massive buildings which have been identified as residences or administrative headquarters of the Persian period have been brought to light. There is no evidence as to where these stood in Jerusalem, and in fact very few objects or pottery that can be ascribed to the period have been found. The written evidence is mainly concerned with factional struggles, in which the fight to maintain purity of religion and race is the main factor.

Even the next stage in the history of Western Asia had little immediate effect on Jerusalem, though its ultimate effect was to convert the eastern Mediterranean littoral into the eastern fringe of a European empire in contrast to a status as the western fringe of an Asiatic one. The event that started this revolution, dramatic in its ultimate result, though slow in effecting the civilizations of the countries concerned, was the battle of Issus in 333 BC, in which Alexander defeated the Persians. In the ten years that followed came the conquest of the whole of Western Asia and Egypt by the Greek armies.

There is no historical or archaeological evidence of any immediate effect on Jerusalem. As so often in imperial wars, the major events took place on the coastal plain, and Jerusalem in the hill-country was left on one side. History is not precise, and archaeology has not so far provided any clear evidence, as to the extent to which these wars had a material effect on Jerusalem. There may have been destructions, and there may have been some deportations of the inhabitants, but archaeologically we cannot pin-point them. The effect of the next century of struggles between Alexander's successors cannot be illustrated.

For Jerusalem, and for the little province of Post-Exilic Judah, an important turning point came in 198 BC when Palestine finally passed into the power of the Syrian Seleucids. Politically, it was important, since for the next century or more the would-be rulers of Jerusalem were able to take advantage of the internal struggles for power amongst the contenders for the Seleucid throne. Culturally, it had the effect of exposing Jerusalem and Judah to the full impact of Hellenism. Judaism had survived exile in Babylon, and its fervent exponents could make no compromise with an alien culture and religion. But an element in the population was won over to the western practices penetrating from the north, and in the thirty years following the establishment of Seleucid power a violent conflict developed between the strict adherents of Judaism and those prepared to accept Hellenistic practices.

The resultant internal dissensions provided Antiochus Epiphanes with an excuse for intervention. In 168 BC he destroyed the city and sacked and profaned the Temple. Almost more resented by the inhabitants, he established a fortress, the Akra of the Syrians, to maintain military control of the city. This Akra was on a site dominating the Temple. Its position has been one of the problems that has long exercised the minds of the historians of Jerusalem. The recent excavations have not so far settled the problem, but the present stage in these excavations suggests that up to this date the higher western ridge was outside the city. Certainly by the first century BC the northern part of it, in the area of the present Citadel and to the south, was within it. My own view is that here was the site of the Akra of the Syrians, and that the construction of this fortress was the first stage in the development of this area which resulted in its inclusion within the city at least by the time of Herod the Great. The completion of the excavations in the area south of the Citadel (Site L on plan,

Fig. 14) may throw light on the problem. So far, one must admit, it is hypothesis only.

The savage Seleucid intervention had the result of the emergence of a strong patriotic party. The Maccabean period is that of the final effort to re-create a Jewish nation, an effort which achieved very considerable success owing to the dissensions within the Seleucid kingdom. Mattatheus took the lead in revolting against the Syrians in 167 BC and his son Judas Maccabeus recovered the city. In the succeeding period, the Maccabean heirs gradually fought off the Syrians and extended their area of rule. Ultimately, the Akra was subdued in 142 BC.

The capture of the Akra marks the culmination of the first stage of the growth of the power of the Maccabees. Their aim at independence from their Seleucid overlords was inevitably opposed. Diplomacy, sieges, tribute, punctuate the succeeding years. But as far as Judah is concerned, the emphasis on an independent state develops steadily. Within Judah, the same development is towards a monarchy. John Hyrcanus, who ruled in Jerusalem from 135–105 BC behaved as if he were a king, though his authentication, as it were, was that by descent he was High Priest.

It is at this stage that one can begin to fit in the archaeological evidence for Post-Exilic Jerusalem to the historical evidence. For the walls of the period of Nehemiah we have evidence at one point, and presumptive evidence enables one to establish their line. For the town inside, we have no evidence, for Roman quarrying and perhaps earlier excavations have removed all evidence. What does survive is additions to the Nehemiah *enceinte*.

Plate 55

Plates 56, 57

The earliest was the tower just south of Site P in Fig. 11. This cannot be precisely dated, and can be a repair of a breach at any time from the fifth century BC onwards. The tower to the south is more precisely dated and is a work of considerable importance. It so impressed the excavators of 1923–6 that it was ascribed to the work of David and Solomon[58]. This it cannot be, since it overlies the remains of houses of the seventh century BC. Its junction with the wall established as belonging to the period of Nehemiah in the 1961–7 excavations has not been excavated, since this would imperil the stability of the area on the crest at this point. But its date could be established by the layers running up to its base. The actual junction of these layers with the base of the tower had been cut by the trench of the earlier excavators. The angle of the slope of the layers left no doubt as to the sequence, and showed that the tower was built in the second half of the second century BC. It could therefore belong either to the time of Simon Maccabeus (143–135 BC) or to that of John Hyrcanus (135–105 BC).

Immediately to the north of the tower is the curious structure which the excavators of 1923–6 called the Jebusite ramp or bastion[59]. It is at first sight a mysterious feature, a great semicircular bulge faced with stepped masonry which provides easy access to the summit, and therefore an odd adjunct to a system of fortifications. The excavators believed it to be a strengthening of the base of the summit defences which they ascribed in origin to the Jebusites, and that it preceded the tower ascribed to Solomon. That it does not belong to this early period is proved by the fact that, like the tower, it overlies the ruins of the seventh century houses. Clearance has also shown that it is not earlier than the tower but later than it. The excavators were however probably right in considering that it was a strengthening of a weak point in the summit defences, as it were a plug in a point of erosion. There is no doubt, from the evidence of excavation in a number of places, that a breach in the summit walls, at the top of the very steep eastern slope could be followed by wash-outs with wide-spread effects. Once an erosion point had been created, subsequent disturbances from torrential rains or earthquakes would tend to concentrate their effects on patches and on the made ground behind them.

Plates 7, 57

Plate 57

Plate 56

The scale of this particular repair suggests that it was to deal with a long-standing and repeated weakness, and in this it was successful. Its nature can be understood in the light of the stratigraphical evidence. The tower stood out as a projection into the steeply-sloping layers that ran up to its foot. The north face of the tower shows an oblique line in the finish of the masonry, sloping up to the existing surface, and continuing the line of the surface shown to be contemporary. The so-called bastion underlies this surface level. It was therefore entirely a substructure, a subterranean buttress to strengthen a weak place in the foundations of the summit wall and covered by the contemporary surface. Its stepped construction, so inviting to attackers, had it been exposed, was firmly buried beneath the steep surface slope.

This tower on the eastern side of the town walls (very probably only one of many strengthenings of the defences), is, for the history of Jerusalem, of lesser importance than developments on the western side. Here there was a deliberate expansion of the city. The summit of the eastern ridge included in the original town was exiguous in the extreme. In the earlier period there had been the extension to the east, made desirable to approach the town as near as possible to the all-important water-supply in the Kedron valley, and artificially built up by an elaborate terrace system. This terrace system had fallen into ruin in the Babylonian destruction, and had been left outside Nehemiah's town. As a result of Hezekiah's water tunnel, the water from the spring was now carried through to the western side of the ridge. When Jerusalem once more began to grow in the Maccabean period, there was no need to recreate the terraces on the eastern side of the ridge, and therefore expansion took place on the easier western side of the ridge.

The most notable example is on the area of Site K. In this area to-day the central valley is constricted and distorted. The excavation of Site K showed that this was the result of an expansion of the summit

Plate 58

46 The only actual houses to survive within the area of the original city were at the top of the eastern slope. They date from the seventh century BC, and were in use down to the Babylonian destruction. They are however founded direct on the stone fill of the terraces constructed in the fourteenth to thirteenth centuries BC *(see* Plates 12 and IV). The reason for this is that the terraces were supported on their outer, lower, sides by retaining walls, which were liable to collapse from earthquakes or other causes, and when they did so, the buildings on the terrace would collapse likewise. All the buildings of the earlier periods have therefore disappeared. On the left is the tower proved to be of Maccabean period, with its foundations on the sixth century ruins (pp. 82–4)

47, 48 The buildings of the seventh century BC, that survived at the top of the eastern slope are not very impressive. The rooms are small and the walls built of rough stones; the walls would however have been faced with plaster, a few traces of which have survived. The staircase, which is a secondary addition, would have led to an upper terrace which has not survived. In the foreground, *below*, was a larger room, only partly excavated. It was of a plan normal at this period in which two rows of monolithic piers supported the roof and divided the room into three. A second pier in this row is seen in Plates 49 and 53, but the other row has disappeared

49 Two of the monolithic piers which supported
the roof of the room in the foreground of Plate 48
are shown surrounded by the debris of the collapsed superstructure. This collapse was the result
of the Babylonian destruction of 586 BC, and
marks the abandonment of this area of the
original city on the eastern slope (pp. 82–4)

50 The domestic character of the houses shown
on Plates 47 and 48 is shown by this oven, which
was found in the narrow room to the left of the
steps in Plate 47. The oven was constructed of clay
and straw, and would have had a domed roof
(pp. 82–4)

51 One of the most interesting finds in the seventh century rooms at the top of the eastern slope was a collection of forty-one stone weights. They are beautifully made, dome-shaped with a flat base. Most are of limestone, often of delicate shades of pink. Twenty-two of them are incised with their weight, mostly in shekels, a few in *payim* or *neseph*. Such a find is exceedingly rare. The Jerusalem weights in fact about double the number known. They range in weight from a quarter-*neseph* with a mass of 2.57 grams, 1.03 cms in height and 1.3 cms in diameter to a giant 24 shekels with a mass of 288.24 grams, 4.45 cms height and 6.3 cms in diameter. The finding of such a large group of weights all together enables useful calculations to be made of the standards in use in Jerusalem; it is likely that there was variation from town to town in this. Allowance has of course to be made for degree of wear, for only a few were in mint condition, and the relatively soft stone would soon show the result of handling. The calculations suggest that there were in fact two standards. It is suggested that when Josiah (638–608 BC) in his reform established 'just weights', the new standards were copied from older ones without allowing for the fact that they were worn, and thereafter a smaller new standard was in use with surviving weights of the old standard (p. 104)

52 One of the problems of excavating in Jerusalem is the immense amount of erosion suffered by all buildings on the slope of the hill. The view illustrates recent erosion channels on the slopes of the eastern ridge above the Kedron valley. The total amount of rainfall in Jerusalem is not very great, and in some years it may fail altogether. But what falls is concentrated in a very short period, and it often falls with great violence. Observation of these modern channels has helped in interpreting phenomena observed in the excavations. These channels were created in 1964, and many of them then appeared at the bases as underground tunnels, up which one could penetrate for a considerable distance. This explained some disturbing observations of areas where, after we had excavated through intact Iron Age levels, suddenly at the base Roman sherds appeared. When investigated these tunnels had suggested what might have occurred, one could trace the wash of a tunnel penetrating through, usually just above bedrock, and introducing the alien material. Violent rain, therefore, played its part in destroying the buildings on the slope, especially those founded on the artificial terraces, to a degree perhaps as serious as did earthquakes. In the next heavy rains in 1966, many of these underground channels were converted into open gulleys, while others were filled up with the silt washed down them (p. 108)

53 A view that shows the disastrous destruction carried out in Jerusalem by the Babylonians under Nebuchadnezzar in 586 BC. The floor of the large room partly excavated at the summit of the eastern slope is buried beneath the rubble of the collapse of the upper part of its walls. This rubble has engulfed two monolithic piers which had formed part of a row supporting the roof. Large rooms divided into a central nave and two side aisles by two rows of monolithic piers are very characteristic of seventh century houses in Palestine. Here, the place where the second row should have come is just where the whole floor of the room has disappeared. The retaining wall of the underlying Jebusite period has collapsed, and in its fall has carried away the whole side of the room. The angle of the debris tipping down the slope is a vivid illustration of how such collapses resulted in the creation of steeply sloping lines of debris running right down the slope in a jumbled mass of stone (p. 84)

54 The wall in the background was built by Nehemiah, who was the Governor of Jerusalem from > 446 to 434 BC. The walls of Jerusalem destroyed by Nebuchadnezzar in 586 BC, had remained in ruins until the time of Nehemiah. In the Book of Nehemiah, a description is given of how he rebuilt the walls in the remarkably short period of fifty-two days. This has been always taken to mean that substantial remnants of the earlier walls survived and that Nehemiah had only to repair them. The 1961–7 excavations have shown that the walls low on the eastern slope were in fact not repaired. Nehemiah, when he made his survey of the state of of walls, found the eastern slope of the hill in chaos as the result of the collapse of the terraces shown in Plate 53. He therefore decided to abandon this whole area, and to build his wall on the crest of the eastern ridge, as here shown. The stonework below left, is an excavation revetment to strengthen the edge of the excavation (p. 111)

55–57   The wall of Nehemiah on the crest of the eastern slope remained the wall of Jerusalem until the destruction of the original city by Titus in AD 70, with frequent repairs and strengthenings. The wall itself is seen in the foreground of Plate 55, and the three different faces of the wall show two rebuildings. These it was impossible to date as the area to the rear had been cleared in the 1923–5 excavations. Contemporary with the second rebuild is the tower shown in Plate 55. This was built over midden tips which contained pottery of the fifth–fourth centuries BC. The much bigger tower further south is shown in Plates 56 and 57. This was ascribed in the 1923–5 excavations to the work of David and Solomon, but was proved in 1961 to be built over the ruins of houses destroyed in 586 BC. The original surface running up to it is shown in Plate 56. Pottery and coins beneath the surface proved that it was built in the second century BC. It was therefore the work of one of the Maccabean rulers of Jerusalem, and was one of the additions to Nehemiah's wall. The tower itself was added to by an extension to the south; the end of the original tower is shown by the straight joint immediately to the left of the upper survey pole. On the right of Plate 57 is seen the so-called Jebusite ramp, which is in fact a bolstering up of the base of a rebuild of the wall, and the view shows that it was later than the tower (pp. 114–6)

58, 59 The western side of the eastern ridge is bounded by the Tyropoeon valley, which is very largely silted up by debris that accumulated after the destruction of Jerusalem by Titus. In the view, *above*, the centre of the valley is beneath the trees at the foot of the ridge in the foreground, and the modern surface at this point is only *c*. 7.25 metres below the summit of the ridge in the background. The original western crest of the ridge is the line of the higher terrace in the background, marked by the line of houses that follow it to near the top left-hand corner of the view. The face of the rock scarp is visible at places, including just beside the small house in the middle distance on the right, where the higher terrace begins. Up to the Maccabean period, this was the line followed by the western wall of the town. It has nowhere survived, for the whole surface of the rock has in most places been destroyed by quarrying, but three areas excavated at the foot of the scarp show that the slopes of the ridge were outside the original town. It was only in the period of the revived prosperity of Jerusalem under the Maccabees that any attempt was made to compensate for the loss of area resulting from the exclusion of the eastern slopes of the ridge, *opposite*. Since, with the existence of the Siloam Tunnel it was no longer necessary to extend the town near the spring, the new expansion beyond the limits of the summit was made on the easier slopes of the central valley. The expansion consisted of terraces built out against the foot of the summit scarp, in principle like the earlier terrace on the eastern slope, but much more solid in construction, *opposite*. In the area shown, *above*, the extension was from the position of the house in the middle distance on the right to a corner that lies between the electric light pole and the poplar, a distance of *c*. 38 metres. The made ground of this terrace was supported on a system of massive substructure walls, seen *opposite*, which were based on a rock and survived to a height here of *c*. 6 metres. The wall on the right proved to be the town wall bounding the terrace (pp. 114–34)

60, 61   Jerusalem from the east today is dominated by the great platform built by Herod to provide
the space for the courtyards of his enlarged temple. On this platform now stands the Moslem sanctuary
of the Dome of the Rock. The views show how magnificently the south-east angle stands out above
the steep slope of the Kedron valley. It was against this angle that Warren sank the remarkable shaft
which is shown in Fig. 12, while Fig.13 shows that beneath the present surface it continues down
another 24 metres to rest on rock. The internal level of the platform is about 3 metres below the top
of the wall. On the left of Plate 60 is the so-called Tomb of Absalom, certainly not earlier than the
third century BC, and perhaps as late as the first century BC. It stands on the opposite side of the
Kedron valley to the Temple (pp. 141–2)

62　Herod's temple platform was built of magnificent masonry, which is shown here in detail. The blocks are enormous, the headers being up to 5 metres long, and the courses mainly 1.25 metres high, but in one case 1.8 metres high. The faces of the stones are beautifully dressed, with a flat boss and a slightly sunk margin *c.* 15 cms wide. The jointing is very close and exact. As the view shows, the face of some of the blocks has been eroded by weathering, but some are still nearly perfect. It is a style of masonry quite new to Palestine, and characteristic of the Herodian period. One is tempted to think that, as was the case in the buildings of Solomon and Omri, foreign masons were imported for the work. At the south-east angle, the Herodian masonry survives to within 6 metres of the top of the wall, as can be seen in Plate 61, that is to say, to a total height of *c.* 41 metres. Another section of Herodian masonry visible today is on the west side of the platform, in the area known as the Wailing Wall (*see* Plate IX and p. 142)

63 Amongst the more interesting finds in Jerusalem of the period of the Kingdom of Judah were a number of handles of storage jars bearing stamps impressed before firing. Such jar stamps are found on a number of sites, and the ones here illustrated come from Tell Duweir, the Biblical Lachish where they were found in houses destroyed in 698 BC. The jars bear the inscription 'For the King', and were presumably connected with the collection of taxes. They also bear the names of a number of towns, Hebron, Sokoh, Zeph and the like, which were perhaps tax entries. The Jerusalem finds came mainly from one group, belonging to the earlier part of the seventh century BC

65   A view over the Old City looking east from near the Church of the Holy Sepulchre. In the background is the Mount of Olives and its continuation to the north, Mount Scopus; the tower on the
skyline is that of the Augusta Victoria Hospital. Beyond the roofs of the houses of the Old City is the
north end of the enclosure of the Haram esh-Sherif, occupying the area of the platform of Herod's
palace. Where the high buildings at the northern end stand was the site of the fortress Antonia, built
by Herod to replace the earlier fortress that had for long guarded the northwest angle of the Temple.
It is very probable that it was in the Antonia that Herod sat in judgement on Jesus, and from here the
traditional *Via Dolorosa* runs to the Church of the Holy Sepulchre. The site of the Antonia is also
important as the east end of the north wall of Jerusalem at the time of the Crucifixion. Evidence from
the present excavations suggests that the wall turned south on a line in the foreground

<   64   A view of the so-called Stables of Solomon beneath the courtyard of the Temple platform. The
buildings consist of vaulted halls, which support the surface of the platform. The bases of the arches
belong to the Herodian period; Herodian masonry is seen in the lower part of the piers in the foreground.
The upper part is a rebuild of the Crusader period. The original structures belong in fact to Herod's
great rebuilding of the Temple platform. A similar use of underground corridors to support a platform
is seen in his Temple of Augustus at Samaria

66   The western face of the Temple platform is in the same typical Herodian masonry as is seen at the south-east corner *(see* Plates 60–62), though the part exposed is here much eroded by weathering. Bonding into this wall, and in similar masonry, is the spring of an arch, known as Robinson's Arch after its discoverer, Edward Robinson, a nineteenth century explorer of Jerusalem. Warren's excavations found the base of the pier, also in Herodian masonry, which supported the other side of the arch. This showed that the span of the arch was *c.* 13 metres and it can be calculated that its crown was *c.* 27 metres above the level of the rock *(see Fig. 1).* Further north can be seen, beneath present-day houses, another arch (Wilson's Arch) also running west from the Temple platform, of which the complete span still survives. These two arches formed the eastern ends of two viaducts that were built by Herod to cross the central valley and provide direct access from the Temple to the western hill (p. 144)

ridge in the second century BC. Whether it will be possible to associate this expansion more closely with any one of the political periods of successful Maccabean rule will depend on the detailed analysis of the evidence from coins and pottery that has still to be carried out. The area is at present bounded on the east by a rock scarp. That this is the limit of the original site is shown by the fact that nowhere in Site K are there any remains of the Bronze Age or Iron Age; the only exception is some Iron Age II sherds in rock crevasses. It was an area outside the city until the second century BC.

The excavation of this area was an archaeological nightmare. The surface layer provided some 2 metres of wash, sloping steeply to the south and obviously following on the collapse of a major retaining wall in this direction. When the levels beneath the wash were reached, they produced so many massive walls that stratigraphical excavation was reduced to restricted pockets. The basic reason for this complexity eventually emerged. The whole of this area was made ground. For this reason the walls of the successive structures had to have very deep foundations. As the excavation progressed, it became clear that we had to find a massive wall to the west which had retained this made ground. As so often happens in excavation, this was on the very fringe of the excavated area. In the south-west corner was a wall of which we could only reach the base on bed rock, at 10.75 metres below the present surface, in a sounding so restricted by adjacent walls that it could be reached only by a ladder and, to allow space to draw the section, the ladder had to be withdrawn. This wall was initially only uncovered crossing the extreme south-west corner of the square. It was however so obviously a candidate for the position of both a retaining wall and a town wall of the period, that in the final stages, when we could pull back the fill into the excavated area, we made an extension to the west, as far as was possible towards the modern road running down the valley. A width of 3.50 metres was exposed at the point when the limit up to which

Plate 59

it was possible to excavate was reached. A wall on this scale is with little doubt the wall for which we were looking, the boundary of Jerusalem in the second century BC.

Of the buildings in this area added to the central scarp, very little can be said. There were at least two major phases of very substantial foundations, but subsequent denudation had removed all the floor levels. All that can be said is that the buildings were so substantial that it is difficult to believe that they were simply private houses. It may be hazarded as a guess that the new area which must have been created by public undertaking was used for public buildings.

The complete line of this Maccabean encroachment on the central valley could only be established by a succession of deep and laborious excavations in this much silted-up area. They would probably only repeat the evidence of Site K, and show the growth of the town in the Maccabean period. Modern building developments are steadily restricting such further excavation even more than the sheer depth of the deposits has hitherto done.

Important light on the line of the western Maccabean town wall to the north was however given by the excavations of Mr J. W. Crow-foot in 1927[60]. Crowfoot's excavations were the first to plunge down into the silted-up depths of the central valley, the Tyropoeon. Beneath the debris upon which Byzantine houses were built, he found a massive wall and gate, built of irregular masonry. The gate certainly remained in use down to the Maccabean period on the evidence of a hoard of coins, dating to the time of Alexander Jannaeus (103–76 BC)[61]. The coarseness of the masonry inclined the excavator to believe that the gate was originally Bronze Age[62], in fact Jebusite. Now that the evidence is clear from similar structures of very roughly squared stones that such a building style is quite compatible with a Maccabean date, it is unnecessary to suppose that the structures had such an ancient origin. Moreover, now that it has been shown that the western limit of the city was still on the western side of the eastern ridge, Crowfoot's gate can fall very happily into the frame-work of the plan of Maccabean Jerusalem.

To the north of Crowfoot's gate, Site M has been excavated during the recent excavations. This site provided evidence of the same encroachment on the central valley. The full implications of the evidence from this site have not yet been worked out. The present interpretation suggests that there was an initial encroachment, which may link up with Crowfoot's wall. Following on a collapse, there was a recession to the east, which may belong to the early first century AD. The exact chronology is dependent on further work on the finds.

Maccabean Jerusalem is thus represented in the archaeological picture as a period of expansion of the city. This is as to be expected. Jerusalem of the Maccabees was a very different place from the Jerusalem re-fortified by Nehemiah. The major unanswered problem is at what stage did the city expand to include the northern end of the western ridge. This occurred before the period of Herod the Great, for the excavations in the Citadel area in 1934–48[63] showed that there were earlier walls underlying Herod's structures. It is suggested above that this was the area of the Akra of the Syrians which finally capitulated to the Maccabees in 142 BC. It is very reasonable to suppose that it was at this time that the area was incorporated within the city walls. Archaeology has not yet produced any evidence on this point, but there is still the possibility that, when the excavations in Site L are completed, and the finds and evidence examined, it may do so.

Again, the history of the period of the Maccabees has had to be reconstructed from the history of the defences. No intact occupation levels within the city have survived. The material which provides the evidence for the dating of the defences, and for the dating of developments such as the massive constructions on the western flank of the ridge, obviously includes the pottery and other objects of daily use at this time. Unimpressive as the finds in themselves are, they enable one to reach an important conclusion. This conclusion is based on the remarkable contrast between the finds at Jerusalem and the finds at Samaria. At the latter site, from the third and especially from the second century BC, the enormous proportion of the pottery consists of copies of Hellenistic vessels, with the characteristic black glaze of the Hellenistic wares imitated by a black wash; actual imports from Greece or the Aegean are fairly common, but infinitely fewer than their copies[64]. Even such commonplace vessels as cooking pots, casseroles and lamps are based on Hellenistic forms. The contrast with the finds at Jerusalem is absolute. A very few black-glazed Hellenistic vessels or their black-washed copies are found, but their proportion to the general mass of pottery is infinitesimal; the characteristic cooking pots and casseroles based on Hellenistic prototypes are virtually absent. The only slight, and rather surprising, link is that at Jerusalem are found a number of the stamped jar handles showing that wine was imported from Rhodes or other Aegean islands such as Thasos.

One reason for this difference between Jerusalem and Samaria may be that when Samaria was conquered by Alexander's general, a Macedonian colony was established there. No doubt, like other settlers in the province of Samaria, they were fairly rapidly assimilated into its mixed population, but a pro-Hellenism may have been incorporated into the local culture. Yet the main reason was twofold. Ever since Omri deliberately selected the site of Samaria as his capital, the province of Israel was open to influences from the north. Secondly, from the time of the Assyrian destruction of Samaria, the population of the northern kingdom had been mixed, and the tradition of Judaism had become weak. This outward-looking habit could only have been accentuated by the disdainful treatment accorded to them by the returned exiles in Jerusalem. Samaria thus was an easy market for Hellenistic wares.

For the inhabitants of Jerusalem, the maintenance of their national individuality depended on the rejection of foreign culture and of intercourse with foreigners. A pro-Hellenistic element did indeed grow up in Jerusalem at the beginning of the second century BC, as described above. The success of the Maccabean rulers established Jewish nationalism for the next century and a half, and the encroaching wave of Hellenism was thrown back. The finds in Jerusalem, illustrated by the basic domestic pottery, are emphatic evidence of the xenophobic attitude of the people of Jerusalem. The only slight concession was that the people of Jerusalem were apparently prepared to buy wine from the Aegean islands. Even so, the number of stamped jar handles that provide evidence of this trade is negligible compared with those found at Samaria.

VII

Herodian and New Testament Jerusalem

THE MACCABEAN STRUGGLE against the power of the Seleucid rulers of Syria lasted, from its rise in 167 BC, just over a hundred years. The decay of Seleucid rule enabled the Maccabean rulers to achieve virtual independence and re-establishment of a monarchy of Judah. It was throughout virtual rather than acknowledged both because of the residual titular over-lordship of the Seleucids, and because with the Jerusalem community there was very strong opposition to the re-establishment of a secular monarchy.

In 65 BC the whole balance of power in Western Asia was changed by the direct intervention of Rome. The influence of Rome had affected events in Asia for a century and a half previously. In 65 BC Pompey began the absorption of the eastern fringes of the Mediterranean into the area of what was to become the Roman Empire.

The immediate effect in Palestine was to change the direction of intrigue. It was not for another quarter of a century that the full-blown power of the Roman Empire emerged with the triumph of Augustus over his rivals. The competitors for power in Jerusalem took an active part in backing the various competitors for power in Rome. By successful diplomacy, Herod the Great achieved rule of Jerusalem and, as a 'confederate king', independent in internal affairs, of an area almost as large as the kingdom of David, and including the coastal plain. He was the son of the Idumaean (or Edomite) Antipater, who had acted as backbone to the otherwise spineless Hyrcanus, the last of the Hasmonean (Maccabean) high priests, and he claimed the full temporal authority of the Maccabean rulers, though he could never claim their religious position.

The position of Herod the Great in Jewish history is an ambiguous one. He ruled in Jerusalem from 37 BC to 4 BC, and his reign has been described as the final climax of the history of Israel[65]. He was not only a skilful negotiator with Rome, he was also a real Romanophile, wishing to create in his domains cities that could rank with cities in the rest of the Roman Empire. In Samaria he could do so, for the differences between Samaria and Jerusalem have already been mentioned, and in Caesarea he was building a new town on the site of an insignificant haven. But in Jerusalem he had to contend with the opposition of the orthodox Jews against all things foreign, against himself as an Idumaean, against Hellenistic-Roman customs and building styles, against everything that was new and alien. His claim to greatness in Jewish history has therefore this element of ambiguity.

There is however no ambiguity in the position of Herod in the archaeological history of Jerusalem. The remains of his structures are some of the few elements of real antiquity that are visible in the city to-day. It was part of his Romanophil policy to glorify the ancient capital of his kingdom, in which the most important structure was the Temple. The ancient glories of Solomon's Temple had long disappeared, and Solomon's Temple had been succeeded by a structure that was the result of the earnest but poverty-stricken effort of Zerubbabel, upon which subsequent repairs can hardly have improved. Herod aimed at placating his Jewish opponents by building a far more magnificent Temple, and he succeeded in persuading the orthodox Jews to build those portions of the structure in which no non-ritually pure intervention could be allowed[66].

Of the true Temple structure, nothing survives. What does survive is the most striking feature in Jerusalem to-day, the great platform on which stands one of the most exquisite examples of early Moslem architecture, the Dome of the Rock. The Moslem sanctuary on its platform towers over the valley to the east and the city to the west. Plates 15, 16, 60, I, XII, XV

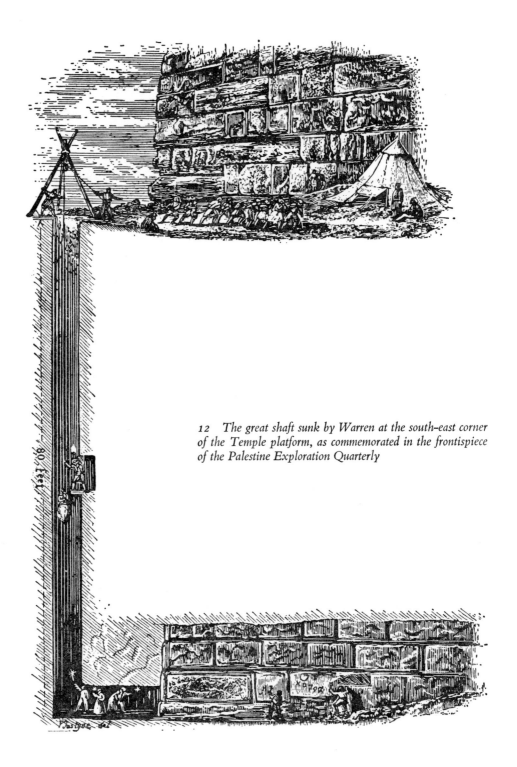

12   The great shaft sunk by Warren at the south–east corner of the Temple platform, as commemorated in the frontispiece of the Palestine Exploration Quarterly

This is bounded to the south by massive retaining walls. Archaeology has shown that the whole history of ancient Jerusalem is based on the levelling up of the steep rock slopes by such retaining walls. Solomon's Temple and its courtyards, and the adjacent royal palace, would only have been made possible by retaining walls with a fill levelling up the natural slope. All this has been engulfed beneath Herod's great structure. It is my own view that the scale of Herod's constructions is such that it is useless to search for the underlying earlier platforms. Equally, I am convinced that such structures once existed.

Plate 15

The platform of Herod's Temple to-day dominates the south-eastern part of the present Old City. Views from the west show it standing up above the close-packed houses which probably do not differ greatly from their predecessors of the first century BC. The full magnificence of the Temple platform can however be better appreciated from outside the town, from the eastern slopes of the Kedron valley. Here, the south-east corner of the platform towers up some 21 metres above the present ground level. To within about 6 metres from the top of the wall, the masonry is Herodian. However, to obtain a true picture of Herod's achievement, one has to have recourse to the records of the excavations in Jerusalem carried out a hundred years ago. When the Palestine Exploration Fund was established in 1865, a veritable pioneer in organized British exploration overseas, it was natural that the first attention of the Fund should be directed to Jerusalem. The Fund commissioned Captain Charles Warren, R. E., later Major-General Sir Charles Warren, to begin explorations[67]. He was severely restricted by political problems and Moslem mistrust, so most of his work was carried out by sinking shafts and tunnels, many of them staggering undertakings that only an officer of the Royal Engineers could have carried out successfully. The most spectacular of all his shafts was at the south-east corner of the Temple platform, an enterprise commemorated in the frontis-piece of the Palestine Exploration Quarterly. From the evidence of

Plate 16

Plates 61, XII

Fig. 12

Fig. 13

this shaft, and of others to the west along the south face of the platform, he showed how the foundations of the wall stepped down
towards the south-east corner to secure a firm foundation on bedrock,
and his section shows that the wall descends some 24 metres below the
modern surface. The total surviving height of Herod's wall is thus
about 40 metres (or 128 feet).

Knowledge of the scientific dating of structures by stratigraphy
did not exist in Warren's time, or indeed for more than half a century
later, and a shaft in any case cannot provide such evidence. Warren
could therefore only conjecture the antiquity of the wall that he
investigated, and many subsequent historians have based conjectures
and theories on his finds. To-day one can be reasonably certain that
nothing that Warren exposed is earlier than the time of Herod. The
platforms of the Temples of Solomon and Zerubbabel have been
for ever encased within the mass of the later structure.

The masonry of this south-east corner is in itself magnificent. The
stones are enormous, and are beautifully dressed, with a flatly tooled
centre, stepped down to a shallow marginal draft. Portions of the

Plates 62, XII

platform wall built in this magnificent masonry are visible at the
south-east corner, and also in the stretch of the western wall of the

Plate IX

Temple platform known as the Wailing Wall, where for centuries
orthodox Jews bewailed the capture of Jerusalem by the Romans.

Herod's Temple platform to-day dominates the eastern ridge of

Plate 67

Jerusalem and equally dominant on the western ridge is his Palace
or Citadel. The present structure takes its origin from Herod's
structure, and its principal tower, known as the Tower of David,

Plate 68

incorporates a remnant of Herodian masonry standing to a considerable height. As has already been said, there is a probability that the
first structure on the northern end of the western ridge was the
'Akra of the Syrians', and that when this fell to the Maccabees in
142 BC, the area was included in the city. Whether or not this hypothesis of the situation of the Akra is correct, it is certain that there was an

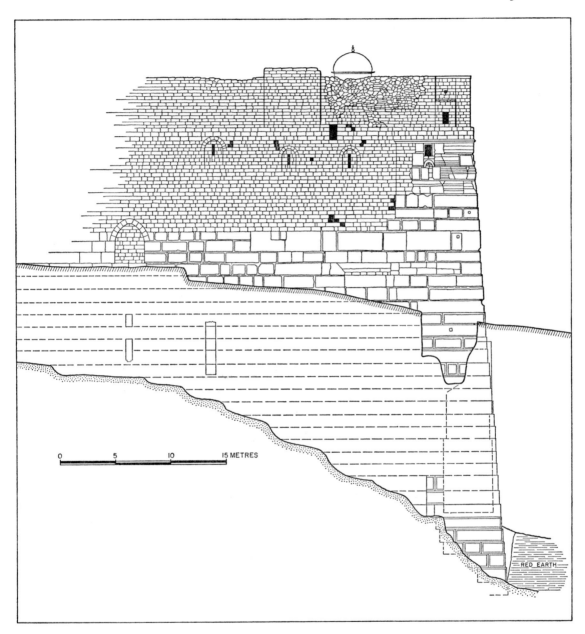

13 The elevation of the south-east angle of the Temple platform on the evidence of Warren's excavations. The large ashlar blocks that survive from within 7 metres of the top at the angle down to rock are Herodian

143

extension to this area within the Maccabean period, for in excavations between 1934 and 1948[68], towers and walls were found underlying those in Herodian-style masonry.

In the Herodian period, therefore, the northern end of the western ridge was included within the city. It is reasonably certain that here was located the Hasmonean palace. Even at this comparatively late period in the history of Jerusalem, the western ridge was divided from the eastern by the deep central valley, the Tyropoeon. Herod's town planning was on such a magnificent scale that he provided for the linking of the royal quarters on the western hill with the Temple area by two viaducts. These have been given the names of their discoverers, Robinson's Arch and Wilson's Arch. Robinson's Arch is visible on the modern surface as the spring of an arch emerging from the Temple platform. Part of Wilson's Arch exists as a complete barrel vault that can be reached by a not too hazardous exploration of the subterranean structures of Jerusalem. It does however require more imagination to visualize them, disembarassed of the medieval structures built against them after the silting up of the central valley, as great free-standing arches crossing the valley to reach the height of the western ridge.

Within Herod's Jerusalem the northern end of the western ridge was thus firmly included. The archaeological evidence is however clear that the southern end of the western ridge was not enclosed by the city walls until the mid-first century AD. The plan of Jerusalem must therefore have been that of an inverted L. There is so far no evidence as to the line of the foot of the L, bounding the southern side of the extension onto the western ridge. On the plan, it is shown as being approximately on the line of the walls of the present Old City, on the grounds that though this was not established until the second century AD, it may have followed a configuration of the ground created by an earlier wall. The only factual evidence is that the extension to the western ridge lies north of Site M.

Plate 66
Fig. 1

Fig. 14

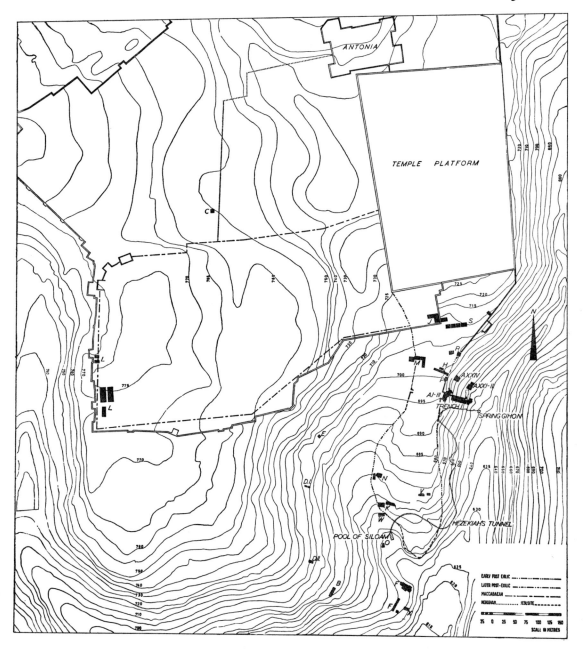

14   Plan of Jerusalem in the time of Herod the Great. There is no evidence for the position of the southern wall of the salient to the west

Herod's Jerusalem is the Jerusalem of the New Testament. Though the actual Temple structure has disappeared, the setting of the courts of the Temple familiar to Jesus is the setting of the Haram esh-Sherif to-day, bounded by the same massive retaining walls. The Citadel and the site of the Fortress Antonia at the north-west corner of the Temple platform can be recognized as the probable sites concerned with the trial that preceded the Crucifixion.

The problem that has exercised Biblical scholars and archaeologists for very many years is that of the sites of the Crucifixion and of the Holy Sepulchre. These sites must have lain outside the contemporary city. To-day the Church of the Holy Sepulchre, covering the traditional sites both of Golgotha and the Sepulchre, is right in the heart of the Old City and to tourists this is very confusing. An answer has to be found to the question of whether these traditional sites can be authentic.

Our evidence starts from the account provided by Flavius Josephus in connection with the Roman capture of Jerusalem in AD 70[69]. Josephus was a Jewish historian, who in the early stages of the rising against Rome commanded a district in Galilee for the Jews. He was however a moderate, to whom the excesses of the rebels in Jerusalem were repugnant, and when he had been defeated and captured, he went over to the Roman side. As a chronicler of the Roman attack on Jerusalem, the climax of the war against the rebels, he wrote as an insider with knowledge of Jerusalem, but with accurate knowledge of the Roman campaign. He describes the final attack of Titus against Jerusalem in great detail, and from this we know that on the northern side, the only side on which steep slopes did not add enormously to the difficulties of the attackers, there were three city walls which Titus had to storm in turn[70].

The innermost north wall he describes as the old wall. It is generally accepted (though in point of fact there is no actual evidence) that this crossed the central valley in a more or less direct east-west line

Plate 65
Fig. 14

Plate 69

from the Temple platform to the Citadel hill, a line approximately that of the present David Street. If the theories put forward here are correct, it would have been Maccabean in origin. The third, or outermost, north wall was the work of Herod Agrippa. Its position on the line of the present north wall of the Old City is described below, but its date, between AD 40 and 44, is irrelevant to the site of the Crucifixion, for it represents a later extension of the city. The crucial wall is the second one. Of this the date is uncertain; it may be the work of Herod, or then it may possibly belong to the late Maccabean period.

Unfortunately, the evidence given by Josephus does not provide us with the details necessary to reconstruct the line of this wall[71]. One end is tied in firmly, for he says it ran from the Fortress Antonia. This fortress was at the north-west corner of the Temple platform, and was built by Herod to take the place of an earlier Maccabean fortress Baris. It was the symbol of the temporal power exercising control over the religious centre. Observations made by Père Hugues Vincent on finds in building operations and chance finds make it possible to draw the plan of Antonia. From Antonia, Josephus describes the second wall running to the Gate Gennath in the old (or first) north wall[72]. Here, unfortunately, we are reduced to conjecture, since there is no evidence as to the position of this gate.

Plate 65

Fig. 15

Most of those who have discussed the problem have considered that the Gate Gennath lies just to the north of the present Citadel. A reasonably direct line from this point to Antonia would lie to the north of the Church of the Holy Sepulchre, and would indicate that the traditional sites were not authentic. An alternative theory would accept the same position for Gennath, but would pick up a number of disjointed finds of ancient walls to make the course of the wall follow a series of re-entrant angles that left the site of the Church outside the walls[73]. A number of military experts have entered the lists to show that topographically this was the better line. A third school of

XI   The area excavated in 1913–14, showing the quarries that have truncated earlier rock-cut cisterns and baths, and have completely removed all occupation levels. The excavation of Site V in the terrace in the upper left-hand corner showed that these quarries were Roman in date (p. 188)

XII   Close-up view of the south-east corner of the Temple platform, showing Herodian masonry nearly to the top (p. 147)

XIII   The area inside the salient of the city wall running south from the Haram in which, in the time of Justinian, two hospices were built (p. 192)

XIV   The trench against the south-east angle of the salient of the city wall in Site S (p. 190)

XV   The Dome of the Rock, the Moslem sanctuary built over the probable site of the Temple. This view was taken before the Dome was plated with gold and many of the ancient glazed tiles replaced by modern copies

XVI   The north walls of Jerusalem as rebuilt by Suleiman the Magnificent in the sixteenth century AD

XI

XII

XIII

XIV

XV

XVI

thought was much more drastic, in suggesting that Gennath lay not at the north-west corner the earlier city, but at a point approximately half-way along the old wall between the Temple platform and the Citadel[74]. These two last alternatives are shown on the plan.

Fig. 15

It was obviously very desirable that any campaign of excavations in Jerusalem should endeavour to throw light on this problem of the Holy Sepulchre. It was fortunate for the Expedition that most of the sites which it was desired to excavate lay outside the present Old City. But any evidence concerning the Church of the Holy Sepulchre could be obtained only from firmly within it, and this presented quite a problem. By the greatest of good luck, in the area of the Muristan, a rather charming formal lay-out of late nineteenth century date, was a vacant site belonging to the Order of St John, part of what was believed to be the medieval Hospitalry of the Order, dating from Crusader times. Permission to excavate here was very readily given by the Order.

When we started to excavate Site C, we did not fully appreciate the difficulties involved. The full extent of the site was only *c.* 30 metres by 15 metres, and its fringes were encumbered by mounds of debris. We found at the onset of the excavation that the top 2 metres of deposit consisted of post-1920 debris. Excavation in the middle of a city has the overriding problem of the disposal of the material excavated. Even though we did at one stage evacuate a considerable amount of the excavated earth and stones (an expensive process when everything has to be transported on donkey-back to the nearest point to which lorries can come, and then carried a mile or more outside the city limits), by the time we could really get down to the business of excavating archaeological levels our area was much restricted. Our final sounding was at its surface only 7 metres × 7 metres and as it turned out, we had to go down 14.75 metres from that level. I must confess that, as the picture was gradually revealed, I had not the faintest hope that we should find the evidence for which we were looking.

Plate 70

Fig. 14

The uppermost structures that we found can be assigned with very great probability to the Hospital of St John. The lowering of level in the new lay-out of the late nineteenth century was however such that all that we found were the foundations of massive piers, forming part of a large-scale vaulted structure. Beneath were buildings of the Arab period, which provided us with a nice collection of the attractive pottery of the period. Below Byzantine and Roman buildings, we reached our real problem. For two solid seasons of excavation, we ploughed through a tremendous fill. There was no doubt that it was a fill, for tip lines ran in every direction. Moreover, it contained a vast amount of pottery of two very different periods, seventh century BC and first century AD.

This fill went on down and down. The only incident that interrupted it was a well-built drain, recalling in structure the Roman drain running down the central valley which is still to-day the main drain of Jerusalem. That this drain was only an incident was shown by the fact that the fill above and below it was of exactly the same character. It was part of the plan that provided for the introduction of this fill.

In an excavation in depth of this sort, in the limited space available, the space for excavation becomes even more restricted by the necessity of leaving access staircases, up which every basket of earth has to be carried. When bedrock was at last reached, the excavation area was only *c.* 4 metres by 4 metres. It seemed quite impossible that what could be found in this space would produce any conclusive evidence.

The fill contained enormous quantities of seventh century BC and first century AD pottery. It was itself 8.25 metres deep and its base was 12 metres from the surface of the intact levels. Then there was a sudden change, and the underlying fill was pure Iron Age, of the seventh century BC. This continued down to bedrock, which was cut in a series of steps and ledges. It is in fact a quarry. This is about the only kind of evidence that could be conclusive as to whether the traditional site of the Crucifixion was authentic.

Plate 71

Plates 71, X

Plate 72

152

Those wanting to quarry stone do not do so within the walls of the town, particularly a close-packed oriental town—they go outside the walls to get their stone. Therefore this area was outside the seventh century BC city. Above the levelled-over surface of the quarry there were no buildings or occupation layers at all until the great fill was put in, at earliest in the first century AD. The context of this fill can be suggested with reasonable certainty. Though the great mass of the latest pottery is of the first century AD, there is just a little that is probably later. It may sound surprising to anyone used to the exact dating that can be given to first and second century pottery in England that there can be any doubt, but dating of pottery in Palestine is not yet as exact as in England. When all our material has been analysed, we shall be in a much better position to make positive statements. There is however a further factor supporting the probability that the fill was not put in until the second century AD. This is the drain, half-way down in the fill, and integral with it. It was clearly part of a major town-planning operation; it had been discovered in a shaft by earlier excavators, who had crawled along it sufficiently far to establish that it was running down towards the central valley to join the great central Roman drain there[75]. The reasonable explanation of the fill is that it was part of the lay-out of Aelia Capitolina by Hadrian in AD 135, when Jerusalem was deliberately blotted out. The process no doubt involved not only the tidying up of the ruins of earlier structures, but the levelling over of hollows to produce a site suitable for the orderly lay-out of a Roman city. As a planned operation, drains were inserted at the required level in the process.

The area of Site C was therefore outside the seventh century town, and remained vacant and deserted until the town-planning operations of Aelia Capitolina. Site C lies directly south of the Church of the Holy Sepulchre, between it and the presumed line of the old, first, north wall which followed approximately the line of the present David Street. Therefore, since it can be proved that Site C was outside the city, the site of the Church must also have been outside. None of the alternative lines for the second north wall based on a position for the Gate Gennath near the Citadel can be possible. The only possible line is the one running to a Gate Gennath in the centre of the first north wall, as shown on the plan. This line leaves both Site C and the Church of the Holy Sepulchre outside the walls.

The evidence is thus clear that the traditional sites of Golgotha and the Holy Sepulchre *can* be authentic, but not of course that they *are* authentic. On this it can only be said that when Queen Helena came to build the Church in the early fourth century AD the site selected was certainly within the Roman city, and the site must have seemed as improbable to her as it does to present-day tourists. The tradition that persuaded her to build on this site must have seemed to her to be very strong.

VIII

The Jerusalem of Herod Agrippa

and the Roman Destruction

THOUGH THE JERUSALEM of the period of the Gospels was the city rebuilt by Herod the Great, native rule, if one can accept Herod as a native, which the orthodox Jews firmly refused to do, ended soon after his death in 4 BC. His kingdom was divided up between his heirs, but such were the dissensions that Rome stepped in, and from AD 6 the greater part of Palestine was governed directly from Rome as a procuratorial province. It is as Roman Procurator, in whose hands was the sole authority of administering the death penalty, that Pontius Pilate appears in the Gospels.

In the rule by alien Procurators there was a brief interval from AD 40 to 44, when Herod Agrippa, grandson of Herod the Great by his Hasmonean wife Mariamne, was allowed by Rome to rule a considerable part of Herod's territories as king. His period of power, which ended with his death in AD 44, was very brief. However, the archaeological evidence shows that his achievements were out of all proportion to the short period of his rule. We know from literary evidence, the account of Josephus[76], that he built a new north wall, the third north wall at the time of the attack by Titus. To the evidence for this, we shall return, but it will be seen that it was approximately on the line of the present north wall of the Old City. What had not been realized until the recent excavations was that he was also responsible for including the southern end of the western hill within the city. From an original site of 10.87 acres, Jerusalem had grown to 140 acres in the time of Herod the Great, and now Herod Agrippa gave it an area of 310 acres.

Fig. 15

Fig. 2

The new wall ran from the south-west corner of the present Old City following the crest of the Hinnom valley, and with the curve of the valley turned east to the place where the Hinnom runs into the Kedron, and then north-east across the mouth of the Tyropoeon to join the original limit of the city at the point of the eastern ridge. This line of wall has long been known. It was traced in 1894–7 by the excavators of the second main Palestine Exploration Fund campaign in Jerusalem, F. G. Bliss and A. D. Dickie[77]. The excavations of Bliss and Dickie make almost as much a saga as those of Warren thirty years earlier. They carried out their work by a series of tunnels, and it was apparently nothing to them to tunnel a hundred yards or so, through deposits filled with fallen stones, incredibly cut through and removed in tunnels only a yard wide, through frequent patches of unsafe ground, and by the light of oil lanterns. Boggle is the only epithet that can be used in one's imagination of their work. In our excavations, we all too frequently came on their tunnels, and greeted them with groans for the disturbances they had created. But when we cleared structures that they had investigated by tunnels, we could only admit that it was hardly necessary to plan them again, for the 'B. and D.' plans were accurate almost to the last detail.

Like Warren, the excavators of the 1890s had not available a knowledge of dating evidence based on pottery typology, and their excavation methods could not provide the stratigraphical evidence upon which this could be based. They knew that they had traced the line of an important town wall, and they interpreted its significance in the light of Old Testament history, discussing its authorship as between the more important of the kings of Judah. Their analysis of the evidence from their excavations remained part of Biblical studies for nearly seventy years.

15   *Plan of Jerusalem in the time of Herod Agrippa*

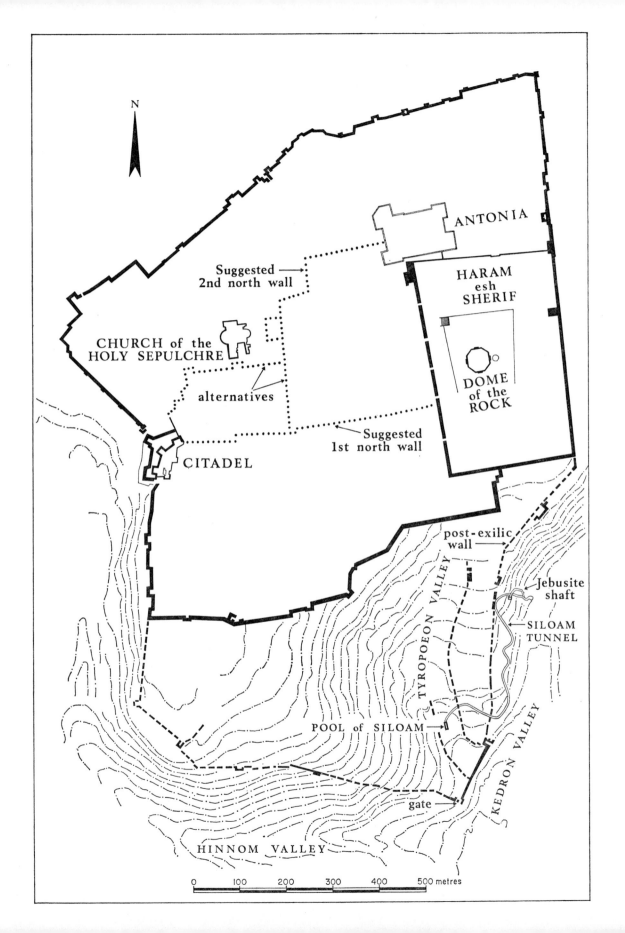

N

ANTONIA

HARAM
esh
SHERIF

Suggested
2nd north wall

CHURCH of the
HOLY SEPULCHRE

DOME
of the
ROCK

alternatives

Suggested
1st north wall

CITADEL

post-exilic
wall

Jebusite
shaft

SILOAM
TUNNEL

POOL of SILOAM

TYROPOEON VALLEY

KEDRON VALLEY

gate

HINNOM VALLEY

0   100   200   300   400   500 metres

XVII

XVIII

XIX

XX

XXI

When the campaign of excavations of the British School of Archaeology was started in 1961, we had no suspicion that the basic Bliss and Dickie conclusions were wrong. Our aim was merely to see if, in the light of our present fairly exact knowledge of the chronology of Iron Age pottery, we could establish which of the kings of Judah was responsible for adding the western ridge to the original Jebusite town on the eastern ridge. Theories ranged from Solomon onwards. Places where the actual wall could be investigated were severely limited by the boundary of the Demilitarized Zone, a no-man's-land between the two successor states, which ran down the crest of the western ridge. Our first excavations, on the absolute edge of the Demilitarized Zone found only the scarp on which the Bliss and Dickie wall had been built. What was surprizing was that all the structures within the area limited by the presumed position of the wall dated only to the first century AD. We proceeded to test the evidence further north, where the Assumptionist Fathers of the Church of St Peter Gallicantu gave us most generous assistance. The sites excavated are shown in Fig. 5. Everywhere the picture was the same, first occupation in the first century AD, down to a date that we at present define as the destruction of Jerusalem in AD 70, followed by a considerably greater development in the Byzantine period.

Finally, we decided that we must re-open the area in which Bliss and Dickie described considerable surviving structures, a gate just north-east of the point where the Hinnom debouches into the Kedron. We uncovered the gate, and we could recognize the 'B. and D.' tunnels. The earlier excavations had removed a good deal of the evidence, but it was possible to recover enough to show that the town wall here was no earlier than the mid-first century AD, and must thus be the work of Herod Agrippa.

Plate 73

The inclusion of the southern end of the western ridge comes thus only in the first century AD. To Herod Agrippa may also belong some of the patches which excavations have shown to have been made to the Post-Exilic line on the crest of the eastern ridge, but the full interpretation of the sequence here depends on a detailed analysis of the finds that has not yet been completed.

The problem of which was the north wall of Herod Agrippa, recorded by Josephus, has been the subject of much debate. Until recently it has been possible to argue between two main candidates, the line of the present north wall of the Old City, and a wall of *Fig. 16* colossal stones crossing the hill some 425 metres to the north. Now the matter has been settled by excavations. In 1965 it was proved that the latter could not belong to the time of Herod Agrippa, while in 1966, the claim of the present wall was spectacularly proved.

Plate 86 The wall to the north of the present city was discovered and excavated in 1925–7, and the excavators came to the conclusion that it was the missing third north wall[78]. It is indeed a most impressive affair on account of the size of stones employed, and of the way in which they are dressed, but in every other way, it is a shoddy construction. The magnificent stones are obviously re-used and battered, and their setting is quite irregular. It could be argued that Herod Agrippa must have built very rapidly, and that shoddy work could be excused on this ground. There was however conclusive dating evidence that the wall was not his work. In the re-excavation of a section of the wall in 1965, it was established that a foundation trench could be traced along the north side of the wall. In the debris, derived from quarrying, into which the foundations were cut, were a number of coins. The latest of these could be dated to AD 54 and AD 59. The wall therefore cannot be as early as the time of Herod Agrippa. Its identification is discussed below.

The excavations against the present north wall were carried out by Dr J. B. Hennessy on behalf of the Department of Antiquities. The Jerusalem Municipality and the Department conceived the magnifi-
Plate 78 cent scheme of excavating beneath the present level of the Damascus Gate to reveal the remains of earlier stages of the gate known to

exist below. The operations involved constructing a bridge to provide access to the present gate, and clearing right down to the base of the wall. The results were spectacular. Below a totally unexpected gate of the Crusader period on a different plan and preceding Byzantine levels, was found an accumulation of the time of Aelia Capitolina. Below that came the original surface and then the foundation trench of the original wall.

The present gate is flanked by two projecting towers which, the excavations showed, followed the lines of towers in the original wall. The lower part of the eastern tower proved to be preserved to a considerable height, and was found to be the finest masonry preserved in Jerusalem. The dressing of the stones is like that of the Herodian masonry at the south-east corner of the Temple platform, but the stones have not been exposed to the elements as the latter have been, and are therefore in much better condition. The base of the tower and the adjacent wall have a projecting plinth, with an excellent moulding surmounting it. It has not been possible to uncover the central arch of the gateway, corresponding to the present gate, but to the north of it the side arch for foot-passengers, flanked by engaged columns, survives to half its height in the original masonry. The whole structure is majestic in the extreme.

Plates 76, 77

Plate 76

A *terminus ante quem* for the original structure is given by the arch just mentioned. It does in fact survive to its crown, but the upper part is very obviously a rebuild. Above the arch in this rebuild is an inscribed stone showing that the rebuild formed part of Hadrian's Aelia Capitolina. A *terminus post quem* is given by the layers cut by the foundation trench. These showed that the wall cannot be earlier than the first half of the first century AD, and therefore it can with great confidence be ascribed to Herod Agrippa.

Of the interior of Herod Agrippa's town, not a great deal has been found. There were a number of structures on the eastern slopes of the southern end of the western ridge, but they have not been excavated over large enough areas for much idea of their lay-out to be obtained. At the southern end of the western ridge, and particularly on the slopes above the central valley, there is a complicated succession of structures, mainly concerned with the extremity of a great dam built across the valley to act as a lower pool for the Pool of Siloam, the present Birket el Hamra. The earliest dam wall probably belongs to the Maccabean period, and it was followed by various structures in the first century AD whose significance has yet to be assessed.

Plate 75

The most spectacular structure that can probably be ascribed to the lay-out of Herod Agrippa's town is a paved street running up the eastern side of the central valley. This was first found by Bliss and Dickie in the excavations of 1894–7[79]. The recent excavations cleared a section of it at Site N. We had become used enough to the 'B. and D.' tunnels on Site F but when we had dug down 6 metres to

Plates 74, 75

reach the street, the significance of a curious hollow was not immediately clear to us. Eventually, however, we realized that it was a 'B. and D.' tunnel which had followed the street from hundreds of yards away, and the plan made in the incredibly difficult conditions imposed by such a tunnel coincided almost exactly with our plan established from the surface.

The street was in itself on a scale to command admiration. It was constructed of magnificent ashlar blocks, in size *c.* 2 metres by 1.50 metres. One can deduce that the buildings that lined the street to the east were similarly imposing. In the area excavated were the jambs of a doorway in true Herodian ashlar masonry. Behind the door-jambs was a great tumble of similar masonry. But what was surprising as excavation proceeded was that there was no floor level onto which the blocks had fallen. In due course it became clear that from the street, through the doorway discovered, a staircase, presumably supported on an arch, had ascended towards the summit of the eastern ridge, climbing over a retaining wall that is probably on the line of the Maccabean extension of the summit area into the central valley. In the collapse, to which we shall return, the stones of the superstructure had fallen into the hollow under the staircase. The collapsed stones included great slabs similar to those used in the street, so presumably another street or important paved area existed at the head of the stairs.

Plate 81

Only twenty-six years intervened between the death of Herod Agrippa and the final destruction of ancient Jerusalem. After his death, Jerusalem was once more ruled by Roman procurators. Their record is one of increasing violence, cruelty, dishonesty and disregard for the things that the Jews held sacred. It is true that we know of their record almost exclusively from Josephus, who, as a Jew, was not unprejudiced. At any rate the inhabitants of Judaea were roused to rebellion. In AD 66 open warfare developed, which moved to its climax in the capture of Jerusalem in AD 70. The war against the Jews was entrusted by Nero in AD 66 to the future Emperor Vespasian, who steadily subdued Galilee and the outlying parts of Judaea. In AD 69 Vespasian was proclaimed Emperor by the Roman troops in Asia, and in AD 70 he returned to Rome to establish his claim. It was left to his son Titus to reduce Jerusalem.

Reference has already been made to the Roman attack from the north and to the three north walls that had to be penetrated. Successively, the three north walls were captured and the Temple, defended by strong walls in its own right, was captured, looted and burnt. The final stronghold of the defenders, the massive towers of Herod's palace or Citadel, was then captured. The whole assault lasted from spring to autumn of AD 70; by September resistance ceased.

Plate 80

The capture of Jerusalem is recorded in Rome by Titus's Triumphal Arch, in which the sacred objects from the Temple are carried in procession, with the leading Jews as prisoners. In Jerusalem, it is recorded as desolation. From literary evidence we know that the walls were breached and destroyed, that the Temple went up in flames, and that the only part of the major structures that survived

Plate 82

Plate 86

Fig. 16

were the three towers of Herod's palace on the northern end of the western ridge, and a portion of the city wall to the south, where the garrison left by Titus was established.

At this point, it is necessary to consider where in the history of the last stages of ancient Jerusalem the wall of colossal blocks north of the present Old City fits in. It has already been shown that it is later than the period of Herod Agrippa. All the pottery evidence shows that it must belong to the first century AD. It must therefore be concluded that it belongs to the time of the capture of Jerusalem by Titus. One's impression on the evidence of the portions visible to-day is that the wall faces south and not north; the face of dressed blocks is 1.75 metres lower on the south side than the very rough foundations on the north side. Unfortunately the removal of evidence by the modern street on the south side deprives one of the confirmation of a contemporary surface. Various theories supported by those who have not accepted the claims of the first excavators that this was the wall of Herod Agrippa have suggested that it was an outwork thrown up by the Jews in the AD 66–70 revolt or in the Second Revolt of AD 130–135. Though the contemporary surface has been removed by modern clearance, none of the reasonably numerous finds of coins or pottery in the recent excavations would support a date in the second century AD. Moreover, the very scale of the work does not accord with an enterprise of hard-pressed defenders. The Jews in the First Revolt were divided into bitterly-opposed factions until the moment of the final attack. An operation on this scale, a wall *c.* 4.50 metres wide, of enormous blocks, running for a proved distance of 375 metres, and almost certainly considerably longer, would have been quite beyond their powers. Even apart from the chronological improbability, it would likewise have been beyond the power of the weaker rebels of the Second Revolt.

The probability therefore remains that it is the work of the Roman attackers. One's first inclination was to suggest that it formed part of

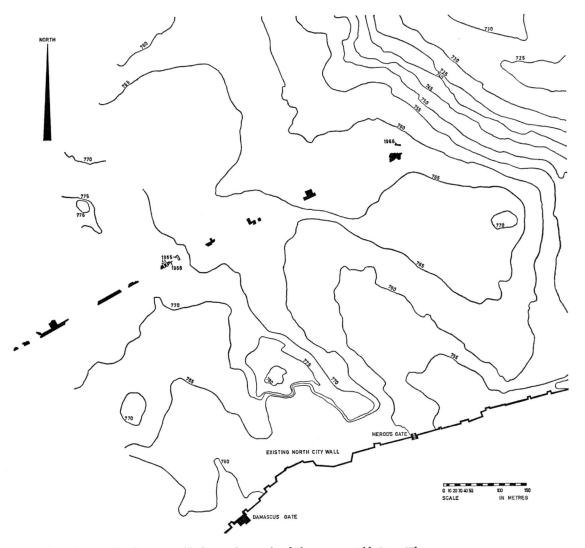

16 Plan of the wall of massive blocks to the north of the present Old City. The most probable explanation is that it is part of the works of circumvallation constructed by Titus during the siege of AD 70

the perimeter of the headquarters of the Xth Legion Fretensis, left by Titus to control the situation after the capture of Jerusalem. The ground for this view was the probability that ashlar blocks of the scale and standard of those incorporated in the wall would not have been available until Jerusalem was destroyed. This is a very real point but one that could be met by the argument that there were blocks ready dressed in quarries for the completion of works begun by Herod Agrippa, or that there were extra-mural structures of great magnificence, such as the Tomb of Queen Helena of Adiabene.

On the whole, the evidence against the wall forming part of the *enceinte* of the Roman legionary quarters seems to be preponderent. In the first place, legionary fortresses had a stereotyped, rectangular plan. The proved extent of the wall in question impinges too nearly on the curve of the eastern valley for any rectangular lay-out to be possible. Secondly no remains that can be possibly attributed to the late first-early second century AD have been found to the north of the wall. Though modern clearance may have removed much of the evidence, it is unlikely that no trace would have survived. All that has been found to the north is a considerable number of graves, clear indication of an extra-mural area.

The probable interpretation of the wall is that it is part of the circumvallations which Titus, on the evidence of Josephus[80], built round Jerusalem to enclose the besieged population, and that for this he used stones from quarries or extra-mural monuments. Problems remain, including the course of the circumvallation round the east and west sides of the city, without which it would have been ineffective, but further investigation may reveal it.

Meanwhile, the literary evidence that the fortress of the Xth Legion Fretensis was established in the neighbourhood of the towers of Herod's palace, which form the basis of the present Citadel, can be accepted. There seemed to be a good possibility that material evidence would be revealed in the area, marked Site L on the plan, in which the Armenian Patriarchate very kindly allowed us to excavate. The very great number of tiles bearing the stamp LEG. X. FR. or its variants, far in excess of those found elsewhere, did indeed suggest that the legionary headquarters was in the neighbourhood. However, the area proved to be terribly disrupted by denudation, presumably due to

Fig. 14

67   Dominating the western side of the Old City today are the towers of the Citadel, flanking the Jaffa Gate, which led to the road to the coast and to Hebron. These towers incorporate towers of the Herodian period, and excavation has shown that beneath them are fortifications of the Maccabean period. By this latter period, therefore, the northern end of the western hill had been incorporated in the city, joined to the Temple by the wall that Josephus calls the First or Old North wall; the line of this probably ran from the right handtower on a line approximately marked by the higher buildings in the left middle distance. The Maccabean period is the earliest at which it can be said with certainty that any part of the western ridge was included within the city; it still remains just possible that the extension was made within the period of the Kingdom of Judah, and the completion of the excavation in the area south of the Citadel is needed to provide conclusive evidence. It is suggested *(see* p. 113) that on the eastern slope of this hill was the site of the Akra of the Syrians, built by Antiochus Epiphanes in 168 BC, to dominate the city, and not captured by the Maccabeans until 142 BC. The site of the Akra then became the palace of the Hasmonean (Maccabean) dynasty. To this royal residence on the western hill, Herod the Great added his own palace, in the north-west corner of the city walls. Josephus describes the magnificence of the palace in great detail, and in particular the towers that defended its northern end, today represented by the towers of the Citadel (p. 142)

68 In this closer view of the towers of the Citadel, the Herodian masonry of the right-hand tower can be seen up to a height of the creeper that partly covers it. Today the tower is erronerously known as the Tower of David. It can be identified with the Tower Phasael, the largest and strongest of the three towers built by Herod at the north end of his palace. The other two, Hippicus and Mariamne, have disappeared (p. 142)

69 The Church of the Holy Sepulchre is built over the traditional sites both of Calvary and of the Holy Sepulchre. The first church dates from the time of Constantine the Great, c. AD 325, and was built under the patronage of his mother, Queen Helena. Little of this church is visible today, but it can be extensively traced below ground level. The most important rebuilding was in the Crusader period when the Christians ruled Jerusalem in the twelfth century AD. The Crusader building established the essential form of the present church, but its plan has been much mutilated and confused by later repairs and additions. It was seriously damaged by the earthquake of 1927, and the scaffolding visible in this view dates from this period. As the photograph shows, it is closely surrounded by other structures which makes a comprehension of its plan and any archaeological investigation very difficult (pp. 146–51)

70   The only open area in the neighbourhood of the Church of the Holy Sepulchre is the site shown
here, Site C, some 150 metres to the south. The upper part of the area was much encumbered by
debris of very recent date. Intact archaeological levels were only reached at the level of the lower ledge
shown in the central area. Much of the area available had therefore to be occupied by the dump. The
archway on the right of the view leads through into David Street. The trees beyond this archway, on
the south side of David Street mark approximately the line of Josephus' 'old' north wall, which is
believed to run from the Citadel to the Temple platform on approximately the line of David Street.
The line that is suggested for the north wall at the time of the Crucifixion by the excavation of this
site would enter this view on the extreme left edge, where the flat white roofs cut the margin of the
photograph. This would therefore be the position of the Gate Genneth to which Josephus said the second
north wall ran. As can be seen, there is no possibility of excavating this area (p. 151)

71, 72 As can be seen from Plate 70, the area available for excavation in Site C was severely restricted. As excavation was carried on down, the area was still further restricted by the necessity of leaving access staircases. As a result the area cleared to bedrock was only *c.* 7 metres by 7 metres. The upper part of the fill consisted of levels of the Arab and Byzantine periods. The photograph shows that at a depth of 4 metres there is a sudden and marked change, with the tiplines of fill clearly visible. There is a break in the layers where the upper figure stands. This is the point at which a massive drain was inserted. But the fill above and below this point is continuous in character, containing a mixture of pottery going down into the second century AD. It was a fill inserted when the city was rebuilt as Aelia Capitolina *c.* AD 135. Only at the very base was there a change, with a seventh century BC fill overlying the quarried bedrock shown in Plate 72. There is therefore a very strong presumption that this area was outside the walls at that date, and remained outside them till the second century AD. The site of the Church would likewise have been outside the walls (pp. 151–3)

73, 74   The expansion to include the southern end of the western hill belongs to the time
of Herod Agrippa, AD 40–44. At the southernmost tip of the western ridge, at the
junction of the Hinnom and Kedron valleys, was a gate, first excavated in 1893–6.
The reclearance that enabled it to be dated to the first century AD is here shown.
On the left and right are the tunnels by which the earlier excavators, Bliss and Dickie,
traced the walls. The same excavators had also tunnelled along the street shown in Plates
74 and 75, and the curve in the right foreground is the roof of their tunnel. The street runs
up the central valley, and has magnificent paving stones more than 2 metres long

75   To the right is shown the foundations of a staircase, which had a doorway of typical Herodian masonry, that led up from the street over the top of the wall in the background to an upper terrace. In Plate 74 is shown part of the terrific tumble of stones that was found covering the street and the whole adjoining area. This represents the destruction of Jerusalem by Titus in AD 70. The whole of this part of Jerusalem was left in ruins, not to be reoccupied for some three hundred years, and the tumbled debris was churned up by winter torrents coursing down the valley (pp. 161, 165)

76–78 The Damascus Gate is the main entrance into the Old City from the north. In its present form it was built by Suleiman the Magnificent in the sixteenth century AD. Beneath lie the gates of the period of Herod Agrippa, mid–first century AD, and the Roman city of Aelia Capitolina of AD 135. These have been revealed by the decision of the Municipality of Jerusalem and the Department of Antiquities to build a bridge to carry modern traffic, thus leaving visible the earlier remains beneath. In Plate 76 is seen on the left the tower built by Herod Agrippa and on the right the eastern pedestrian entrance of his triple-arched gateway. The detail of the magnificent masonry of the base of the tower is seen in Plate 77. The arch of the gateway was flanked by two engaged columns which were mutilated when an Ommayad cistern was built against it. The upper part of the archway is in different masonry, and is shown to belong to the period of Aelia Capitolina by an inscription on the stone above the keystone of the arch. The gate was therefore rebuilt after the destruction of Jerusalem by Titus in AD 70; a possible alternative is that the gate of Herod Agrippa was never finished and the upper masonry represents a completion rather than a rebuilding. The slight distortion of line in Plate 76 is due to the joining of two photographs, made necessary by the cramped space within the excavated area (pp. 162–4)

79, 80 In the ruins shown in Plates 74 and 81 was found a hoard of twenty coins of the First Revolt of the Jews (pp. 135–6). The revolt was provoked by the growing oppression and cruelty of the Roman procurators who, after the death of Herod Agrippa, ruled Judaea. It was a final outbreak into violence of long-simmering resentment, developing into open defiance of Rome in AD 66, and spreading from Jerusalem throughout the province of Judaea. A force of 60,000 men under the future Emperor

81 A vivid illustration of the destruction of Jerusalem is this tumble of stones in Site N. Here is seen the collapse over the staircase shown in Plate 75. The giant paving stones, similar to those used in the street at the foot of the staircase, presumably came from an upper street or terrace. This destruction of Jerusalem in AD 70 was the work of Titus, who was left in command of the Roman forces when his father in AD 69 returned to Rome to secure his position as Emperor. The final siege took six months

Vespasian was sent to restore order. Vespasian devoted his attention first to reducing the outlying regions and Jerusalem was left to itself. It was in this period that the coins of the First Revolt were struck. The illustration (of coins in the British Museum) shows, above, the obverse and reverse of a *shekel* of year 1, and, below, the obverses of *shekels* of years 2, 3 and 4. The revolt ended with the capture of Jerusalem by Titus in AD 70, and *above* is shown a *sestertius* of Titus with the legend *Judaea Capta*

82   When the city at last fell, Titus carried off thousands of prisoners and great booty. On his return to Rome, he was given a Triumph, and the details of the procession as recorded on the Arch of Titus, still stand in Rome. In the view here shown, the sacred vessels and fittings of the Temple are shown carried in the procession, noticeably the golden table that stood in the Holy of Holies and, most prominent of all, the seven branched candlestick or *menôrah* (p. 165)

83, 84 In AD 135, following the Second Revolt of the Jews, Hadrian proceeded to obliterate Jewish Jerusalem by building on top of it Aelia Capitolina. The position of the north wall of Aelia beneath the north wall of the present Old City, has long been known, but that of the south wall was only established in 1966. These views, Plate 83 from the east and Plate 84 from the west, show the salient that projects south from the Temple platform, then turning to form the south wall. The lower courses are of enormous blocks in a very distinctive style, not found elsewhere. Excavation in the adjoining area showed that this was built as the south wall of Aelia, and that the area outside was used as a quarry to provide building stone (pp. 189–90)

85 In a trench against the angle of the salient shown in Plate 83, the wall was shown to have been built on rock immediately below the present surface. Beneath the wall, the rock was cut in a vertical scarp, continuous with the face of the wall. This scarp was part of a vast quarrying operation, for at its foot, as shown in this view, it cuts into the roof of a cistern. Clearly the scarp was cut after the wall was built or at least planned. The date of the wall can thus be bracketted between that of the By-zantine period, to which belong the levels over the quarry, and that of Herod Agrippa, whose town extended much further south. It must therefore belong to Aelia (p. 190)

86 The position of the north wall of the time of Herod Agrippa has been much debated. One can-didate is a wall excavated in 1925, of enormous blocks, clearly re-used in their present position. Coins of AD 54 and AD 59 found in 1965 showed that the wall was later than the time of Herod Agrippa. It was probably part of the circumvalla-tion works that Titus is known to have constructed to prevent the defenders breaking out during the siege of AD 70 (pp. 166–8)

87 After the destruction of AD 70, Jerusalem lay in ruins for more than sixty years, watched over by the Xth Legion Fretensis, encamped on the western hill. But the opposition of the Jews to the Romans had not been crushed, and it came to a head in the Second Revolt in AD 130. There is no historian of these events to provide a record such as Josephus provided for the First Revolt. It is clear, however, that the Jews claimed to set up an independent kingdom since coins were struck dated by the year of the revolt. These coins *(tetradrachms* in the British Museum) belong to years 1 and 2, while one, right, is not dated. Two bear the name Simon, the leader Simon Bar-Kochba, evidence of whose last stand in the southern wilderness has recently been found in caves

88 The Byzantine period in Jerusalem was one of great prosperity. After Christianity became the official religion of the Roman Empire, the city became a place of pilgrimage, where pious benefactors built many churches. The surviving archaeological evidence of the period is, however, very fragmentary. The most famous church is that of the Holy Sepulchre, built early in the fourth century (*see* Plate 69). An especially active builder of churches was the Empress Eudoxia, who lived in Jerusalem from AD 443 to 460. Probably to her period belongs a church of which the terribly fragmentary remains were found in Site L, for an inscription on a fragment of a mosaic floor (*see* Plate XVIII) suggests it was built by the noble lady Bassa, one of her entourage. This view shows in the centre the only part of the structure to survive, the foundations of an apse at the east end. The rest of the foundations have been robbed out. Subsequently the remaining fragments were built over by the walls of the Mameluke period (*see* Plates 91, 92 and pp. 190–91)

89, 90 An area in which considerable fragments of the foundations of Byzantine buildings survive is Site M (Plate 89). The growth of prosperity in the Byzantine period led to expansion south of the walls of Aelia, spreading once more over the area of the town of Herod Agrippa. In the view here, the floor has been removed, and the walls are seen built directly on the tumble of stones marking the destruction of AD 70. In Plate 90 is seen the northern wall of an important building, built in the area (see Plate XIII) between the Temple platform and the salient shown in Plate 83. At the top is a paved street that ran along the foot of the Temple platform. The building probably formed part of two hospices built by Justinian (AD 527–565) for foreign pilgrims and for the indigent sick (p. 192)

91, 92 The only large area available for excavation within the Old City was in the Armenian Quarter in the south-west corner of the walls. Here was found an important building of the Mameluke period, of the fourteenth century AD. In the upper view can be seen the parallel walls that supported three vaulted halls. The lower view shows smaller rooms, built originally in the Byzantine period, and incorporated into the Mameluke structure. The building was probably a caravanserai belonging to the people of Hebron (p. 196)

the proximity of the wall crowning the steep slope to the west. Remains of the Roman period were found, but nothing sufficiently coherent from which a military lay-out could be deduced. The completion of the excavations in this area may produce more evidence, but it is possible that the legionary headquarters lay further to the north, between Site L and the present Citadel.

The recent excavations have provided striking evidence of Titus's destruction. The absence on the whole extent of the eastern ridge of any structures between the first century AD and the Byzantine period could be the result of clearances at later dates, but it cannot be accidental that in all the wash-layers down the eastern slope, pottery and coins stop abruptly in the later first century AD. There was no occupation on the summit to be washed down the slope and in Site K the break was clearly defined. The final structures were regularly planned houses, beneath which was a well-built drain, a lay-out of a sophistication that suggests Roman influence, and the pottery agrees with a date in the mid-first century AD. It was a lay-out that culminated in the period of Herod Agrippa. These remains are the latest in the area. In the destruction of these buildings, walls were razed, paving stones torn up, and the drain clogged with material firmly dated to the last part of the century by the pottery. In the drain were human skulls and other bones, washed down from the ruined city higher up the slope.

Fig. 14

Even more dramatic were the finds in Site N, the area in which the fine street of Herod Agrippa was uncovered. Reference has already been made to the collapse of the staircase leading east from the street (p. 165). The tumble of stones was remarkable even for Jerusalem where tumbles of stones are a phenomenon all too common in excavations. The magnitude of the disaster perhaps made a special impact owing to the excellence of the destroyed buildings as shown by the magnificently-dressed stones, and the period of the collapse was very precisely pin-pointed by the discovery at its base of a hoard

Plates 74, 81

cf. Plate 79

of coins of the First Revolt, hidden by defenders who could not recover them before the city was overwhelmed by Titus. Even more indicative of the complete desolation of this area that had formed part of the city of Herod Agrippa was the state of the ruins. The fallen masonry blocked the central valley, the Tyropoeon. When the ordered lay-out of the cities of Herod and Herod Agrippa, with the drains and retaining walls which controlled the forces of nature, was destroyed, the central valley reverted to its natural function. Torrents of water from winter rains swept down the valley. The stratification of Site N showed how these torrents had churned up the debris resulting from the destruction by Titus. It was two centuries or more before human activity began once more to make its mark in the whole area of ancient Jerusalem.

IX

Roman and Byzantine Jerusalem

WHEN TITUS DEPARTED after his capture of Jerusalem in AD 70, the city was in ruins, and the Xth Legion Fretensis was left to control the ruins. The dispersed Jews continued however to be a thorn in the side of the rulers of Rome. The Emperors Trajan (AD 98–117) and Hadrian (AD 117–138) had to deal with risings; the main centres of these risings were in the areas to which Jews had been dispersed ever since the Babylonian destruction of the sixth century, but the centre of all Jewish aspirations was Jerusalem. Whether Hadrian's decision to obliterate Jerusalem by the establishment of a Roman city on top of it was the cause or effect of the Second Revolt of the Jews, is uncertain, for there is not available for this stage the literary evidence that Josephus provides for the First Revolt. It can certainly be argued that it was part of Hadrian's policy to build new cities in parts of the Roman Empire stretching from Asia to Britain. At any rate, when the desperate efforts of the rebels had been quelled by AD 135, Roman Jerusalem, Aelia Capitolina, was established.

Plate 87

As far as the recent excavations are concerned, our first visual impression was of the whole-scale approach to this lay-out of a Roman city above the ruins of its predecessor. The 8 metres deep fill in Site C, with its incorporated evidence of town-planning in the drain, shows how the problem was tackled. Parts of the ruins were razed, parts of the area were levelled up, and then the Roman city was laid out.

Plate 71

The north-south axis of the city so laid out is visible to-day in the street running slightly west of south from the present Damascus Gate, and in the Byzantine mosaic of Madeba this is shown as a columned street, the chief north-south street of a classically-planned town; the bases of some of these columns have been found in the vicinity of the Church of the Holy Sepulchre. That the main north gate of the town was on the site of the Damascus Gate is shown by the inscription above the rebuilding of the Herod Agrippa gateway. The north wall of Aelia Capitolina thus followed approximately the line of the present north wall of the Old City.

The evidence for the abandonment of the whole area of the original city on the eastern ridge, accumulated in the early days of the recent excavations, made it clear that the limits of Roman Jerusalem must lie to the north. It was, however, only in the excavations of 1966 that clear evidence as to the actual line of the southern limit of Aelia Capitolina emerged.

Fig. 14

Later quarrying has been given several times already as the reason why none of the buildings of the original city and its successors on the summit of the eastern ridge have survived. Excavations in Site V showed that this quarrying was initially carried out in the Roman period, though it was supplemented by Byzantine quarrying. Site V immediately adjoins the large-scale clearance made by M. R. Weill in

Plate XI

excavations on behalf of Baron E. de Rothschild in 1913–14[81]. The rock surface as so revealed shows the drastic truncation of innumerable rock-cut structures, cisterns, baths, and two tunnel-like structures which have been identified as royal tombs, though my own view is that this is improbable. All deposits and buildings above the rock were ruthlessly removed over a large area in this quarrying to obtain building stone. The extent is shown by the outline of a cistern on the summit of the ridge; the rock to the south of it was removed to the extent of at least 5 metres. The excavations in Site V showed that this operation belongs to the Roman period, and the obvious context is the need for stone to build Aelia Capitolina. The Roman city not only buried those parts of the earlier cities which lay within its area, but in most of the area outside its limits the very basis of earlier Jerusalem was cut away.

A good deal of the area available for excavation north of Site V had been cleared by earlier excavators. The probability is that nearly all the structures exposed by them belong to the post-quarrying Byzantine period. At any rate, in those areas in which excavations have been carried out in the campaign starting in 1961, the effect of the quarrying can be seen.

Disastrous for evidence concerning the early history of Jerusalem as is this quarrying, it does at least provide evidence for the south wall of Aelia Capitolina. As the plan shows, the present south-east angle of the Old City is formed by the angle of the Temple platform. At a distance of 180 metres from this angle, a salient runs south for a distance of 90 metres, and thence the wall turns west to form the main south wall of the Old City. The masonry of the original wall of this salient is very impressive. In the scale of the blocks it rivals the Herodian work in the Temple platform, but the style of the dressing of the blocks is entirely different, with very rough and heavy protruding bosses. The date of this salient has long been uncertain. A *terminus ante* was given in Site J within the angle, an area in which we were unfortunately prevented from completing the excavations. It was however proved that a later stage of the wall belonged to the time of the Arab Caliph Abd el Aziz, *c.* AD 975, and beneath that there were Byzantine structures that can be assigned to the period of Justinian in the sixth century AD.

Fig. 15

Plates 83, XIII

Plates 84, XIV

The area bounded by the south wall of the Temple platform, on the west by this salient, and on the south and east by the modern road into the city by the Dung Gate was one very inviting for archaeological examination, for it is unencumbered by modern buildings. Eventually in 1965 we were allowed to begin excavations here, by permission of the supreme Moslem religious authority, the Awqaf, and the valuable intervention of the Department of Antiquities.

Plates 83, 84

The excavation in this area is not yet complete, but the evidence is already clear as to what we can expect. We shall not find any

Plates 85, XIV

evidence of the first extension of the original city northwards by Solomon, to join it to his Temple. The area will certainly be proved to have been quarried for Aelia Capitolina. This evidence has been provided by a trench against the east face of the south-east corner of the salient. It proved that the salient wall was built on rock almost immediately below the present surface, but it also shows that this rock had been cut away on a vertical face immediately below the face of the wall. Either the wall was already there when the scarp was cut, or it was at least planned. The scarp continued down for 5 metres and at its base cut into the roof of a cistern; it therefore added very appreciably to the height of the wall, and the probability is that the rock quarried away provided part of the stones for building the wall. The levels that subsequently accumulated over the quarried surface were Byzantine. The wall must therefore come between the time of Herod Agrippa and the Byzantine period, and thus fits perfectly as the wall of Aelia Capitolina.

There is not much likelihood of finding out a great deal about the interior of Aelia Capitolina. From time to time isolated fragments, drains, cisterns and the like, have been revealed in modern structural work. Immediately east of the Church of the Holy Sepulchre, work in connection with the Russian building uncovered some substantial walls, which have been preserved, and which may form part of a monumental entrance from the columned street to a Roman temple reported to have been built on the site of Calvary. Beneath the Convent of the Sisters of Sion to the north of the road leading in from St Stephen's Gate, part of a triumphal arch of the Hadrianic period is visible[82]. In a few places portions of Roman structures protrude above the modern surface, but the closely built-up modern town makes it impossible to obtain a coherent history of the Roman city. Great hopes were based on the permission by the Armenian Patriarch to

Fig. 14

excavate Site L, the one large open space within the Old City just inside the south-west corner of the walls. It proved however that the area is so near to the line of the ancient west wall that successive destructions of this wall must have resulted in severe wash-outs down the steep slope to the west, similar to those found on the eastern slopes. Almost the whole of the deposit, at least 10 metres deep and still deepening to the west where the excavations are not yet complete, consists of a series of great water-made gulleys, filled up again with gravel and wash. At the base a few fragments survive of the foundations of buildings of the Roman period, but so far not enough has been recovered to give much idea of the plan.

Our knowledge of the history of Aelia Capitolina is, like that of the plan, exiguous. But the picture changes with the Byzantine period. When Constantine made Christianity the official religion of the Roman Empire in AD 313, Jerusalem acquired a world-wide importance that it has never lost. Pilgrims flocked there, and their accounts give pictures of varying clarity of the city. The greatest monument of the Byzantine period was the Church of the Holy Sepulchre, built by Queen Helena, mother of the Emperor Constantine, *c.* AD 325. Advantage is being taken of the current restoration of the structure, being carried out jointly by the various religious communities which share its ownership, to study the Constantinian remains, a study to which Père H.-M. Couäsnon, O. P., architect of the Latin community, is giving special attention. When the work is completed, we shall know as much about the first church as the complex later buildings will allow. Other churches in Jerusalem proliferated in the next century, especially under the Empress Eudoxia in the mid-fifth century AD. Since the main object of the present work is to describe the information provided by recent excavations, the positions and descriptions of other churches derived from literary evidence or that of earlier excavations are not here discussed. The only contribution made to the picture of probably vast ecclesiastical activity is a find of some fragments of walls and a portion of a mosaic in Site L. The walls are horribly mutilated by the gulleys already described, that

Plate 69

Plate 88
Plate XVIII

have destroyed all the deposits in this area down to the thirteenth century AD. The surviving fragments are apparently part of the three-apsed eastern end of a church. In the northern side-apse was a most attractive mosaic in which a hare and a four-footed beast are set beneath the shadow of a tree. An inscription suggests that the church may be part of a monastery built by the patrician Lady Bassa, one of the entourage of the Empress Eudoxia.

Such was the prosperity of Jerusalem in the Byzantine period that it started once more to expand to the south, beyond the limits of Aelia Capitolina, and over the area occupied by the earlier cities. Eudoxia is credited with enclosing this area within a new city wall, and the probability is that this followed the line of the southern wall of Herod Agrippa. Over much of this area the recent excavations have found buildings of the Byzantine period. All those that can be identified seem to form part of private dwellings. On the eastern ridge, and over the debris that had filled up the central valley after the destruction of AD 70, the earlier ones are substantial in character.

Plate 89

Good examples are seen in Site M. On the western ridge, in the rather limited area examined, they seem to be slighter, and to incorporate caves used as dwelling places.

The most substantial Byzantine buildings excavated, and one which is certainly public in character, lies within the area of Aelia Capitolina,

Plate XIII

in the south-east angle of the salient created by the wall of this city, which is described above (p. 189). Here, excavations have revealed portions of what may well be the two adjacent hospices constructed, according to Procopius, by Justinian (Emperor AD 527–565), one for foreign pilgrims, one for the indigent sick. Between these buildings

Plate 90

and the Temple platform was a paved street, and between the higher level of this street and the lower levels of the hospices was a massive retaining wall flanked by a columned portico.

The decreasing prosperity of the last years of Byzantine Jerusalem

Fig. 14

is shown by the upper levels in Site S. The buildings in the upper levels are miserable and increasingly sparse. The find of the only gold coin that the recent excavations have produced provides an illustration of the desperate position of Byzantium that is perhaps unintentional. It is a coin of Heraclius, the last Byzantine ruler of Jerusalem. He stands flanked by his sons Heraclonas and Heraclius Constantinus, an impressive figure with wonderful handlebar moustaches, breathing defiance in every line. The date of the coin is AD 629/30. But Heraclius's defiance was unavailing, and in AD 636 Jerusalem fell to the Arab advance that was sweeping through the ancient classical world.

Plates **XX, XXI**

X

Islamic and Crusader Jerusalem

Plates I, XV

Fig. 14

THIS CHAPTER is a brief epilogue to the main story, not because of the lack of interest and importance of the period, but because excavations have contributed little material for it.

By AD 691, Jerusalem began to take on much of its present appearance, with the completion of one of the most beautiful buildings in the world, the Dome of the Rock, in the centre of Herod's Temple platform. Similarly, Arab buildings were taking the place of their predecessors all over the city, not changing it very much in character, for many of the craftsmen and builders were Byzantine-trained. Buildings of the Byzantine and early Arab period were excavated in Site C, south of the Church of the Holy Sepulchre, and the evidence of the appearance of Ommayad pottery was necessary to show us that we had passed from the one period to the other. An Arab bathing establishment could equally well have been Byzantine, and a Byzantine mosaic floor was incorporated in a succeeding Arab building.

Site C shows a bigger break with the appearance of the Crusaders, when the First Crusade put the rule of Jerusalem in the hands of the West for nearly a hundred years, AD 1099–1187. The area became part of the Hospice of the Order of St John of Jerusalem, and the massive foundations of the piers of the vaulted building were cut through the underlying Arab and Byzantine levels. Unfortunately, the clearance carried out in the area in building operations of the late nineteenth century had removed its floors. All over the city the brief period of Crusader rule must have been one of considerable building activity, especially as regards church building. The contributions of the Crusaders to the complex building of the Church of the Holy

Sepulchre are emerging like those of the Constantinian period as the present restoration is progressing. The Dome of the Rock and the adjacent Mosque of Omar became Christian churches, and elsewhere new churches were built or older buildings refurbished.

The excavations that have made the greatest addition to our knowledge of the Crusader period are those carried out outside the Damascus Gate on behalf of the Department of Antiquities, under the direction of Dr J. B. Hennessy. As described above, p. 162 ff., the purpose of the clearance was to expose the Roman structures at the base of the present wall and gate. It was a complete surprise that at a depth of 2·75 metres a building was reached, of which the ecclesiastical character was shown by wall paintings on fallen blocks; part of a dado belonging to the decoration was still in position on one wall.

Plate XIX

The building lay outside the present walls, to the west of the gateway. Its date was undoubted, for it was built over a reconstruction of an Ommayad cistern, and cut into innumerable road surfaces dated by Ommayad coins. Overlying it was the debris beneath the gateway of the sixteenth century AD; it could only belong to the period of Christian rule between AD 1099–1187. It was first interpreted as an extra-mural chapel, perhaps for the use of lepers who were forbidden entrance to the city. However, as clearance was continued, it proved not to be outside the wall at all. For a reason that is at present obscure, a great outwork was constructed here to the north of the Roman gate. Some 20 metres north of this gate is a very massive wall; for the most part only the core of the wall survives, but the few facing-stones in position show that it was an impressive structure. From beneath the present gateway, a paved road runs between flanking structures and turns east to run along the inside of the massive wall. In this return to the east is the threshold of a gateway. Clearly, then, in the Crusader period the actual gateway was set forward in advance of the Roman gate, and was planned with a right-angled approach behind an outer wall of which the extent is not yet known. In the

Plate 78

area to the west of that part of the approach running north from beneath the present gateway was the ecclesiastical building, and now that we know that it was inside and not outside the walls, it can be identified as the Church of St Abraham, known to lie just inside the Damascus Gate. Much of the entrance with its right-angled turn is being preserved *in situ*, though across it has to be carried a bridge to provide access to the present gate, and the lay-out is complicated by the need to leave visible the magnificent footings of the tower and gateway of Herod Agrippa 6·10 metres below.

The only other considerable contribution that excavations have made to the later history of Jerusalem belongs to the period when Islam once more ruled Jerusalem, after the reconquest in AD 1187 with the expulsion of forces of the First Crusade, and after the brief episodes of the Sixth Crusade in AD 1229–39 and 1243–4. For this period, Site L at last provided structures on a scale commensurate with our hopes for such an inviting open, level space. After the disastrous wash-outs which had successively carried everything, Byzantine, Roman, Maccabean and perhaps earlier remains, down the slope to the west, the wall built in the Mameluke period appears to have survived such perils, for it must still retain the terrace on which the Mameluke building is preserved on an imposing scale. It consists of three great vaulted halls running north and south, and flanked on the east by small rooms and to the west by a street or lane. The masonry is solid in the extreme. Part of it was built in the Mameluke period, but at each end of the central hall structures on a considerable scale of the Byzantine period were included. It is reasonably certain that

Plates 91, 92

we can recognize in these halls the caravanserai of the people of Hebron, known to have existed in this area. In it would have stayed the people of Hebron when they came to Jerusalem to visit the sacred centres in the Haram esh-Sherif, or to sell their produce to the people of Jerusalem.

To Suleiman the Magnificent is due much of the present appearance of the Old City of Jerusalem. In AD 1538–41, he rebuilt the walls of the city, and it is his walls that for the most part enclose the city to-day. The uppermost courses belong to later repairs, but his masonry can be seen in the lower courses for almost the entire circuit; the Damascus Gate to-day looks much as it did in the sixteenth century. We know now that, at least at key points on the north and south, Suleiman's wall follows the line of the walls of Aelia Capitolina. The lay-out of this city so moulded the contours that its effect is seen through two millennia. For instance, when in the Byzantine period the city extended once more to the south, the salient running south from the Temple platform (referred to above, p. 189) still remained a dominant feature, for we have found that the sixth century AD buildings inside it are not less than 11 metres higher than the sixth–seventh century buildings outside it to the east. At least by the time that the Caliph el Aziz rebuilt the walls of Jerusalem during his reign beginning in AD 975, the line had reverted to the line of the walls of Aelia Capitolina. There may be deviations in some areas; about the northwest angle in particular we know little, and it has been inaccessible in the Demilitarized Zone. These deviations are not however likely to be important.

Jerusalem to-day therefore received its form in AD 135. Almost the only link with the form of Jerusalem of New Testament times is the great platform of the Temple built by Herod the Great. Visible links with Old Testament Jerusalem are non-existent, though a Temple platform must have dominated the city from the time of Solomon in the tenth century BC. Roman quarrying on the surface of the hill and the effects of man and nature on the slopes have removed most of the internal buildings of ancient Jerusalem. Archaeological examination, however, starting a hundred years ago, down to the campaign begun in 1961, has at least succeeded in tracing the outlines of the successive towns, and we can therefore now claim that we have available some material for a picture of the town in which the events of the Old and New Testaments took place.

Plates I, XVI

Plate 78

Notes

Numbers in italics, other than Biblical references, refer to the Bibliography, pp. 202–203.

Chapter I

1   *20a*, pl. XXVI.
2   *20a; 20b.*
3   *2.*
4   *20a.*
5   *3a.*
6   For the latest study, see *Cambridge Ancient History*, Revised edition, Vol. II, Chap. XX.

Chapter II

7   *20a; 20b.*
8   *8.*
9   *8*, p. 57.
10   *2 Samuel 5.6.*
11   *2 Samuel 5.8; 1 Chronicles 10.6.*
12   *7.*
13   *19a.*
14   *1 Kings 1. 32–40.*
15   *2 Samuel 5.9; 1 Chronicles 11.8.*
16   *1 Kings 9.15; 2 Chronicles 32.5.*
17   The various references to *Millo* and the interpretations that can be put upon it have been discussed by, amongst others, Simons in *16*, p. 132 ff. It would be out of place here to discuss the problem in detail, but the repair of these terraces does seem to fit the problem of interpretation in the different passages.

Chapter III

18   *2 Samuel 24.16.*

19   *19b*, pp. 588–9.

20   *3b*, pp. 5–9.

20 a The season's excavations carried out after this was written did, in fact, prove that Solomon's extension was on the crest only. The extension north on this slope came in the eighth century BC.

21   *12*, pp. 17–18.

22   *23a*, pp. 11–14; *23b* pl. CI.

23   *22.*

24   *9.*

25   *23a*, pp. 11–14; *23c*, p. 83; *23b* pls. CXX–CXXIV.

26   *18, passim.*

27   *1*, p. 209.

28   *3c.*

29   *10.*

30   *10, e.g.* I pp. 139ff; II p. 520 and pl. VI; p. 509, fig. 413.

31   *2 Kings 6, 23–28.*

32   *3c*, pls IV and V.

33   *10, e.g.* p. 549, fig. 482; p. 561, fig. 504.

34   *1 Kings 9. 15, 19; 2 Chronicles 8.6.*

35   *23e; 23d.*

36   *6*, pp. 151–2.

Chapter IV

37   *2 Kings 12.3.*

38   *2 Kings 14.4.*

39   *2 Chronicles 26. 16–21.*

40   *2 Kings 20.20; 2 Chronicles 32.30.*

41   *19a*, p. 42; *2 Kings 25.4.*

42   *2 Chronicles 32. 3–4.*

43   *21.*

44   *2*, chap. V.

Chapter V

45 *15.*

Chapter VI

46 *2 Kings 25.23; Jeremiah 40. 5–6.*
47 *2 Kings 24.14.*
48 *Ezra 4. 6–24.*
49 *Haggai 2.18.*
50 *Ezra 6.4.*
51 *Nehemiah 2.13.*
52 *Nehemiah 2.14.*
53 *Nehemiah 3.*
54 *Nehemiah 6.15.*
55 *Nehemiah 3. 13–15.*
56 *Nehemiah 3. 21–22.*
57 *8.*
58 *8*, p. 57.
59 *8*, pp. 51-2.
60 *3a.*
61 *3a*, pp. 15 and 104–5.
62 *3a*, p. 17.
63 *4.*
64 *3d*, pp. 217–81.

Chapter VII

65 *13.*
66 *5a*, XV. xi. 2.
67 *20a, 20b.*
68 *4.*
69 *5b*, Books V and VI.
70 *5b*, V. iv.
71 *5b*, V. iv. 2.
72 *5b*, V. iv. 2.
73 *19b*, pp. 90–113.

74 *16*, pp. 295–309.
75 *20b.*

Chapter VIII

76 *5b*, iv. 2.
77 *2*, chaps. I–III.
78 *17*, p. 51ff.
79 *2*, pp. 140–47.
80 *5b*, V. xii. 1-2.

Chapter IX

81 *21.*
82 *11.*
83 *14*, V. 6.

Bibliography

Abbreviations

A.J.A.   *American Journal of Archaeology*
A.P.E.F.   *Annual of the Palestine Exploration Fund*
B.A.   *Biblical Archaeologist*
I.E.J.   *Israel Exploration Journal*
O.I.P.   *Oriental Institute Publications*
P.E.Q.   *Palestine Exploration Quarterly*
Q.D.A.P. *Quarterly of the Department of Antiquities of Palestine*

1   BARNETT, R. D., The Nimrud Ivories and the Art of the Phoenicians, *Iraq II*, 1935.

2   BLISS, F. J. and DICKIE, E. C., *Excavations at Jerusalem 1894–1897*. London 1898.

3 a   CROWFOOT, J. W., *Excavations in the Tyropoeon Valley, Jerusalem 1927*, *A.P.E.F. V*. London 1929.

   b   —, KENYON, K. M., SUKENIK, E. L., *Samaria-Sebaste 1. The Buildings at Samaria*. London 1942.

   c   — and CROWFOOT, G. M., *Samaria-Sebaste 2. Early Ivories from Samaria*. London 1938.

   d   —, CROWFOOT, G. M., KENYON, K. M., *Samaria-Sebaste 3. The Objects from Samaria*. London 1957.

4   JOHNS, C. N., Recent Excavations at the Citadel, *Q.D.A.P. XIV*, 1950.

5 a   JOSEPHUS, FLAVIUS, *Antiquities of the Jews*.

   b   — *Wars of the Jews*.

6   KENYON, K. M., Megiddo, Hazor, Samaria and Chronology, *Bulletin 4 of the Institute of Archaeology*. London 1964.

7   LAMON, R. S., *The Megiddo Water System. O.I.P. XXXII.* Chicago 1935.

8   MACALISTER, R. A. S., and DUNCAN, J. G., *Excavations on the Hill of Ophel, Jerusalem, 1923–1925. A.P.E.F.* London 1926.

9   McCOWN, C. C., Tell Tainat, *A.J.A.* 1937.

10 MALLOWAN, M. E. L., *Nimrud and its Remains.* 2 vols. London 1966.

11 MARIE ALINE, SOEUR, *La Fortresse Antonia à Jérusalem et la question du Prétoire.* Jerusalem, Jordan, 1955.

12 MARQUET-KRAUSE, J., *Les Fouilles de 'Ay (Et-Tell) 1933–1935.* Paris 1949.

13 NOTH, M., *The History of Israel.* London 1958.

14 PROCOPIUS, *De Aedificiis.*

15 SCOTT, R. B. Y., The Scale-weights from Ophel 1963–64. *P.E.Q.* 1965.

16 SIMONS, J., *Jerusalem in the Old Testament.* Leiden 1952.

17 SUKENIK, E. L., and MAYER, L. A., *The Third Wall of Jerusalem.* Jerusalem 1930.

18 TUFNELL, O., INGE, C. A., HARDING, L., *Lachish II. The Fosse Temple.* London 1940.

19a VINCENT, L. H., *Jérusalem sous Terre.* London 1911.

  b — and STEVE, A. M., *Jérusalem de l'Ancien Testament.* 2 vols. Paris 1954 and 1956.

20a WARREN, C. and CONDER, E. R., *The Survey of Western Palestine. Jerusalem.* London 1884.

  b WARREN, C., *Underground Jerusalem.* London 1876.

21 WEILL, R., *La Cité de David.* 2 vols. Paris 1920 and 1947.

22 WOOLLEY, C. L., *Alalakh.* Society of Antiquaries of London. Research Report no. 18. London 1955.

23a YADIN, Y., Excavations at Hazor 1957, *I.E.J. 8*, 1958.

  b —, ET ALII, *Hazor III–IV.* Jerusalem, Israel 1961.

  c — Excavations at Hazor 1958, *I.E.J. 9*, 1959.

  d — New Light on Solomon's Megiddo, *B.A. XXIII*, 1966, p. 62 ff.

  e — Solomon's City Wall and Gate at Gezer, *I.E.J. 8*, p. 80 ff. 1958.

List of Illustrations

All photographs, with the exceptions noted, were taken by the photographers of the 1961–7 excavations, Miss N. Lord, Miss C. Western, Peter Dorrell and Ian Blake, and the copyright belongs to the Jerusalem Excavation Fund. The copyright of the other plates belongs as follows: 1 Elia Photo Service, Jerusalem; 4 Staatliche Museen, Berlin; 17, 79, 80, 87 Peter Clayton; 18, 19, 27 Palestine Exploration Fund; 21, 22, 23 Professor Y. Yadin, the Hebrew University, Jerusalem; 24, Trustees of the British Museum; 25, 26 Professor M.E.L. Mallowan and the British School of Archaeology in Iraq; 28 Oriental Institute of Chicago; 41 Palestine Archaeological Museum; 63 Trustees of the late Sir Henry Wellcome; 64 Miss C. Western; 76, 77 Dr J.B. Hennessy; 78 Alistair Duncan; 82 Mansell-Alinari; to all of whom the author is grateful for permission to reproduce.

204

Figures

The plans are the work of the expedition's architect, Brian Johnson, with the exception of Figs. 1, 2, 12, 13 which are reproduced by permission of the Palestine Exploration Fund. The drawings of objects are the work of successive artists of the expedition.

Index

Numbers in italics refer to plates